Patricia Gallimore's
organic YEAR

A GUIDE TO ORGANIC LIVING

ACKNOWLEDGEMENTS

This book could not have been written without the help, advice, encouragement and support of the following people, to whom I offer my greatest thanks: all the people whose farms, homes and businesses I visited during my research, and whose stories appear in these pages, and their families and staff who gave me so much time and hospitality, including many memorable organic meals; Patrick Holden, Emma Parkin and other members of staff at the Soil Association; Alan and Jackie Gear, who appear in the book but also gave invaluable help and advice before I began to write it, and their staff at HDRA especially Sally Cunningham and Pauline Pears; Lawrence Woodward at Elm Farm Research Centre; Patsy Westcott, Charlotte Lochhead, Emma Shackleton, Lisa Pettibone and the rest of the team at BBC Books for all their kindness to a new author; Nicola Brown for her wonderful photographs; Vanessa Whitburn, Keri Davies, Sue Ward, Camilla Fisher, Jane Pritchard, Louise Gifford and so many others in *The Archers* office; and last, but by no means least, thanks and love to my husband Charles Gardner for his patience and understanding during the writing period, and most of all for the hundreds of miles he drove me during the research so that I could concentrate on my interviews and making up my notes.

Published by BBC Worldwide Limited,
Woodlands, 80 Wood Lane, London W12 0TT

First published in 2000
Copyright © Patricia Gallimore and Patsy Westcott
The moral right of the author has been asserted

ISBN 0 563 55145 3

Soil Association standards have been used throughout the book. They are published in the Soil Association's *Standards for Organic Food and Farming 1999*. Information has been sourced from publications, reports and surveys produced by official bodies such as: Fresh Fruit and Vegetables Bureau, HDRA, MAFF Advisory Committe on Pesticides, Pesticides Action Trust, the Soil Association, Sustain (the National Food Alliance), UK Pesticides Action Network (formerly Pesticides Trust) and UK Pesticides Residue Committee (formerly Working Party on Pesticide Residues). The authors and publisher have made every effort to give accurate information, but organic standards are constantly under review.

Photographs by Nicola Browne

except those on pp 148–9 and 151 © Fairtrade Foundation; pp 152 and 154 Whole Earth Foods; pp 153, 155 and 175 © BBC Worldwide; and pp 176–7 Cephas/Mick Rock. The publishers would like to thank them and Planet Organic, Portobello Wholefoods, Sunnyfields Organic and Wild Oat Wholefoods for the use of their products.

Commissioning editors: Emma Shackleton and Anna Ottewill
Project editor: Charlotte Lochhead
Book design art director: Lisa Pettibone
Designer: Susannah Good
Cover art director: Pene Parker

Set in Syntax and Minion by BBC Books
Printed and bound in France by Imprimerie Pollina s.a. - n° L80207
Colour separations by Imprimerie Pollina s.a.

CONTENTS

INTRODUCTION

I joined the cast of *The Archers* in 1974, and later that year my character, Pat Lewis, married into the Archer family and became Mrs Tony Archer. For the next 10 years Tony and Pat Archer farmed their land at Willow Farm, and later at Bridge Farm, conventionally, working hard but struggling. Tony was always somewhat in the shadow of his sisters, Jennifer and Lillian, both the wives of rich men. In 1984 the production team decided to convert one of Ambridge's farms to organic practice.

At the time 'organics' wasn't the buzz word it has since become, and the concept was still considered by many to be the province of cranks. Most people doubted that organic farming really worked and Pat and Tony, in common with real-life organic farmers, had to endure the ridicule of conventional farmers who thought they'd probably fail and sooner or later return to farming with chemical fertilizers and pesticides. Sixteen years later Pat and Tony Archer are still farming organically – and successfully – in Ambridge, and organic farming has stopped being considered eccentric. Organic farmers throughout the country, convinced that farming without potentially harmful agrichemicals is healthier for the population and the environment, are now reaping the success they deserve.

Since the food scares of recent years, in particular BSE, more and more people have questioned food values and sought out safer food uncontaminated with chemicals and pesticide residues. Organic food is now much in demand and becoming increasingly available through supermarkets, box schemes, farm shops and other outlets.

Farmers' markets, springing up all over the country, are a great source of fresh, locally produced food. In Warwickshire, where I live, an increasing number of stallholders are selling organic produce. I've noticed that others are advertising their meat and vegetables as coming from farms undergoing organic conversion, such is the popularity of organic food. The markets have become increasingly well patronised, the only drawback of shopping there being that it takes longer to get round the stalls as I always meet friends and get talking!

The Soil Association describes itself as the organization which 'exists to research, develop and promote sustainable relationships between the soil, plants, animals, people and the biosphere, in order to produce healthy food and other products while protecting and enhancing the environment'. They provided *The Archers* team of producers and writers with much help and

The 'organics' label

There are strict rules governing the use of the label 'organic'. All food so labelled must by law come from growers, processors or importers registered with a body approved by the government's United Kingdom Register of Organic Food Standards (UKROFS) or a body approved by UKROFS. Always check your product has been approved and labelled by one of the following organic certification bodies:

 Organic Farmers and Growers

 Scottish Organic Producers' Association

 Organic Food Federation

Organic standards are constantly under review, and UKROFS only certify UK-grown or processed food so you may see other European symbols of products. All producers are subject to regular inspections to make sure that they conform to EU regulations and UKROFS standards. The same applies to imported organic food from outside the EU. These include

avoiding non-approved fertilizers or pesticides, practising crop rotation, observing animal health and welfare standards, preserving and enhancing wildlife habitats and the environment, and farming land organically for a conversion period of (usually) two years before selling produce as organic. Regulations also limit what ingredients may be used in processing. For instance, genetically modified

 Soil Association Certification Ltd

 Biodynamic Agricultural Association

 Irish Organic Farmers' and Growers' Association

organisms (GMOs, see p 85) are not allowed and neither is irradiation of food, although manufacturers can use up to 5% of specified ingredients of non-organic origin if alternatives are unavailable. Non-agricultural ingredients like water, yeast and salt are not included at present but this is now under review.

---

advice during the period of Bridge Farm's organic conversion, and they still advise today on all the programme's organic story lines. As a result of playing Pat Archer, organic farmer, dairywoman and shopkeeper, I have been lucky enough to have been invited by the Soil Association, and organic farmers and growers up and down the country, to attend agricultural shows, annual conferences, food and wine festivals, and numerous other events in the 16 years since Pat and Tony went organic. I've had opportunities to meet many of my real-life counterparts, and visited some beautiful parts of the country, which I might not otherwise have discovered. I have met some truly outstanding people in the organic farming world and heard some wonderful stories about people's lives and their reasons for becoming and remaining organic producers. Without exception, the people I have met through the organic world are committed, caring and generous-hearted. None was originally motivated by profit and financial success (though many of them have since achieved it), but by strongly held beliefs about the health and welfare of the countryside, animals and the population. I admire them more than I can say.

During the year spent writing *Organic Year* I have returned to visit some old friends, and made many new ones. Each month I visited a key figure in the organic world, meeting a variety of farmers and producers, and learning a huge amount from the very special people who shared their time with me. This book tells their inspirational stories, and I hope it will be of particular interest to people wanting to discover organic food for the first time, and maybe have a go at growing their own fruit or vegetables organically.

For those new to the idea of organic living the Practical Organics information given each month in the For the Shopper sections aims to highlight what is different about organic produce: why it's healthier to eat organic food, how organic farming differs from conventional farming, and how buying fresh seasonal food and growing your own vegetables and fruit can change the way you eat and live. The What to Try lists illustrate some of the different fruits and vegetables available in the shops each month, not only seasonal home-grown produce, but also imported fruit and veg as well. Imports are indicated with *(i)* to try and show you what's UK produced and harvested at different times of the year, and what's imported. Obviously, because so much is now available all year round, things are changing all the time so you may find differences when you visit your local supermarket. The recipes, at the end of each Practical Organics section, are added to encourage you to use the many organic products, fresh and storecupboard, now appearing in the shops and markets.

The For the Grower sections are designed to point out some of the differences between conventional and organic gardening, and to highlight some of the basic techniques that an organic gardener needs to be aware of. These sections are by no means intended as a comprehensive guide to gardening organically, but are a very basic guide for the first-timer to introduce them to the concept and illustrate what growing organically entails. Maybe these titbits will encourage people to give organic gardening a try, and seek further information from the many excellent books which deal with the subject in detail (see p 190 for some useful reading suggestions).

My organic year has been a truly memorable one. I have Pat Archer to thank for introducing me to the world of organics, and to the many remarkable organic farmers and producers I have met since 1984. I hope that by my telling some of their stories and by giving a few basic guides to organic shopping and gardening, people who may not have tried it before may be tempted to find out more about an organic lifestyle.

january

One of the most influential figures in the organic movement in the UK, Peter Segger is Managing Director of the multinational Organic Farm Foods (Wales) Ltd. He grows organic vegetables and fruit on his farm and is founder and first Chairman of the Organic Growers' Association.

In 1985 Peter and other organic farmers created Organic Farm Foods (OFF) to provide an infrastructure to supply and distribute their produce. With headquarters at the factory and distribution centre at Lampeter, West Wales, there are branches in Honeybourne, Leominster and Scotland, with subsidiaries in the USA and South Africa. Today OFF buys fresh organic fruit and vegetables from all over the world, working directly with organic farmers and growers in 27 countries (including New Zealand, Guinea, Chile, Egypt, Israel and the USA) to supply the markets in the UK, France and the USA. Using the latest temperature-controlled vehicles, OFF delivers to every regional centre in the UK, overnight, seven days a week, in all weather conditions, ensuring the produce's maximum freshness. Their aim is to help develop local markets throughout the world and contribute to a more sustainable trading system internationally; they are totally committed to the organic movement and to the continuing growth of the organic food market through technical development and research. As Peter Segger says in OFF's brochure, 'We are quite simply a totally organic food company – and proud of it!'

When I visited him at his 50-acre farm in West Wales to talk about his work and see where his organic roots were planted back in 1974, I arrived on a bright, frosty January day. I had driven several miles inland from Aberaeron, on

Greenhouse/polytunnels at Peter Segger's farm in West Wales containing the delicate salad veg and crops he produces for distribution daily throughout the UK.

the spectacularly beautiful Cardigan coast and, even in winter, the countryside here is glorious. It is easy to understand what drew Peter (and others) to this area.

Peter Segger and Anne Evans's traditional old Welsh farmhouse was the first of many surprises. Behind the main house there is a recently built extension, and it's one of the most beautiful modern rooms I have ever seen. The huge living and sleeping area is light and spacious, and the abundance of glass in the ceilings as well as the windows makes the most of the natural light. The walls and furniture are pale, natural colours and there are spectacular panoramic views of the gardens, surrounding farmland and woods. Perhaps the greatest delight, though, is the natural, untreated oak, which came from the farm's woodland and has been used with stunning simplicity as supporting beams, floors and doors for the building. The extension has won Royal Institute of British Architecture awards and been featured in magazine articles, but perhaps most important to Peter is the fact that, as he says, 'I feel part of at least a six-hundred-year cycle. The oak had stood in the woodland for at least three hundred years, and this building should with luck last the same amount of time... I'm just here for a small part of it!'

We drank coffee by the blazing wood fire, before a walk round the farm to hear how Peter got into organic farming, and how Organic Farm Foods came to be created. 'I work long hours during the week, and a walk round the farm always rejuvenates me,' he enthused. I felt sure it would do the same for me and, well wrapped and booted, set off with him.

Peter, like so many others in the organic community, not only farms organically but also has a lifestyle that reflects his care and concern for people, animals, the environment and the beauty that nature gives us. He has a garden with a river running through it and has plans to create the most amazing water features, using sculpted geometric-shaped stones called flow forms. They are of varying designs, some looking rather like clubs in a pack of cards, and the water runs through them to create mesmerizing swirl effects. The stones look lovely but, on a practical level, they help to purify the water, too. The garden also has a natural pool where Peter swims in the summer... 'It's wonderful, but always freezing cold,' he told me. He plans to create ponds to encourage frogs, as they are useful to organic gardeners for pest control. Peter has learnt to love gardening, although he admits his busy life doesn't allow him enough time for it, but, as he says, 'Organic gardening is so easy, you don't have to weed as long as you use plenty of mulch, which feeds the soil, and keeps the weeds away – efficient and practical.' Easy!

On the way to the greenhouses (vast, domed, polythene tunnels), there were sheep due to begin lambing any day. They are a cross-bred Île de France–Merino, that produce fine wool, and they are nourished by waste vegetable matter from OFF's processing and distribution factory. OFF has a successful recycling policy, feeding animals the suitable waste vegetables and composting any that are unsuitable. (OFF delivers the waste veg in re-usable containers, and recycles all its packaging materials, too.) Peter is passionate about the health of the soil, from which all things are grown, and is currently carrying out experiments with composting. He explained that scientists really know very little about the soil, but that in just 1 gram there are over 600 million bacteria, and over 40,000 different species. 'We need them all,' he says. 'The soil is constantly changing and, if fed with good natural compost and manure, will remain healthy and organize itself. Chemicals attack good as well as bad bacteria.'

The farm's greenhouses produce a whole range of unusual crops. Grown through black plastic, used for weed control, the tender plants are also provided with warmth. There was a range of salad plants with some

The cross-bred Île de France–Merino sheep play a part in OFF's recycling policy as they are fed on suitable waste vegetable matter from their processing and distribution factory.

exotic red-leafed varieties, lettuce, endive and spinach, and herbs including coriander and parsley. Pak choi and other Chinese vegetables are grown for stir-fry packs that OFF produces for the supermarkets. The farm experiments with unusual varieties that conventional farmers, and those converting to organics, don't grow. Anne oversees this area of the business, and they produce constantly changing varieties and good outdoor, as well as greenhouse, crops for the fast-growing organic vegetable market. Peter is proud that they employ a lot of people and have proved that a good living can be made from just 50 acres. It was this farm along with a co-operative of neighbouring farmers that originally supplied OFF's whole business before it grew to what it has become today.

Over the river is the glorious Welsh woodland that Peter loves so much. He refers to the ancient oaks as his best friends, and pointed out their sheer vitality and the tight-knit branches, which provide so much more wood than the more delicate ash. He is constantly expanding his knowledge of woodland management, and has recently cleared areas to allow in more light and space for new growth. Peter has recently invested in a mechanical chipper so that instead of burning waste wood it can be shredded and turned into valuable mulch.

Peter is keen to promote schemes involving young people, and is considering the possibility of setting up a scheme to employ local young adults to set up a business using wood from his alder copse. Alder is currently being sought as a cheaper alternative to oak for parquet flooring – very popular in Germany especially. One summer, a group of art students were invited to come and create sculptures from wood left over from a clearing scheme. The results are an added delight to the woodland scene and the sculptures range from the weird and the geometric, to a monumental horse's head with stones for teeth which just makes you laugh out loud.

The woods are carpeted in spring and summer with daffodils, bluebells, anemones and orchids, and Peter often comes here to sit after a stressful day

A sculpture in the woods, made by one of a group of art students invited one summer to create works of art from some of the wood left over from a tree-clearing scheme.

in order, as he puts it, to refresh his soul. Nearby, at the top of the wooded hill, is a quarry where stone was gathered for the original farm buildings. By the quarry is a small cottage, dating from 1800, that was once a hill farm. It broke Peter's heart to watch it falling into ruin and, now that they can afford to, they are restoring it. When it's finished he would like it to be somewhere people can come and stay to gain peace and refreshment from these glorious ancient woods.

Peter came to Wales in 1974 and began farming, after some years living in a thatched cottage near Henley-on-Thames, surrounded by farmland. He had watched as fields were sprayed with pesticides and chemicals, and felt instinctively that that was wrong. Government policy at the time was to encourage a big rise in food production, and farmers were persuaded to use chemicals to achieve this. Peter was deeply food conscious, and by now vegetarian, and argued constantly with farmers to urge them to stop spraying. One day, when an exasperated farmer suggested that if he thought he was so clever, why didn't he try farming without chemicals for himself, the idea was planted. He sold his cottage and his share of the frozen seafood import–export business he was running, and raised enough money to buy the farm in Wales and to live for several years.

Peter admits he knew next to nothing about farming, and had to learn from scratch. In those days there were virtually no books available on organic agriculture, so much of his information came from books for gardeners. He remembers especially being inspired by the writings of the

A spring carpet of daffodils in the ancient woodland on Peter's farm.

late, great, organic gardening expert Lawrence Hills (founder of the Henry Doubleday Research Association, see p 57). 'I was a real novice,' he confessed, 'I more or less had books spread out in front of me while I worked!' He once dug an entire field by hand, and by trial and error discovered what worked and what didn't. He enjoyed exploring and experimenting with sometimes unconventional techniques, and felt he had no choice but to do so.

Also in that area of Wales at the time were a group of like-minded young organic farmers and growers. Patrick Holden (neighbouring farmer and now Director of the Soil Association), the late Dougal Campbell (who became Managing Director of Welsh Farm Foods), and Rachel and Gareth Rowlands (whose farm near Aberystwyth had been organic since the 1940s, and who created Rachel's Organic Dairy, see p 25). All were supplying vegetables and salads to local shops and restaurants, delivering over 50 different varieties between them. They saw the potential to expand and develop the organic market beyond Wales and, realizing that their farms were suffering as the result of all the marketing they were trying to take on, they formed a co-operative and set up Organic Farm Foods in 1985.

One of OFF's temperature-controlled lorries operating seven days a week, all year round. They deliver produce to the UK's regional centres overnight to ensure maximum freshness for their organic vegetables and fruit.

Together they created an infrastructure driven by fresh produce, and proved that if you could make a living from 50 acres in Wales, you could do it anywhere. The business started by employing six people, and in the first week they sold half a ton of potatoes, three-quarters of a ton of cabbage and a quarter of a ton of carrots. The produce sold fantastically, and when they ran out of local Welsh vegetables they began buying from England. Later, as the market continued to expand, importing was instigated. Today OFF employs over 300 people and distributes around 1700 tons of fresh produce from all over the world every week. The Lampeter factory now, once again, deals mainly in Welsh produce, with the other factories dealing with the imports and exports.

The original co-operative in Wales worked hard, not only for the organic movement as a whole, but also for each other. Patrick Holden and Gareth Rowlands were producing milk, which in those days had no organic premium, so Dougal Campbell, a cheesemaker, created a soft Brie-type cheese called Pencarreg to use up the milk. When, shortly after the co-operative had been set up, Peter broke both legs, the others took over the running of the farm and Peter, on his crutches, was able to run the vegetable marketing side of the co-operative. Anne pointed out, too, that an unsung hero at this time was the bank manager in Lampeter, with whom many of the group had their accounts. He believed in them, and agreed to loans to enable the expansion of their business, even if, as Peter says, 'We all had our farms in hock in those early days.'

Peter was invited to join the council of the Soil Association (see p 100), the country's leading organic organization, in 1979 as a result of the work he was doing. The Association had been founded in 1946 by a group of forward-thinking farmers, nutritionists and scientists who were concerned about intensive farming methods adopted after the Second World War to push the land into greater productivity. Many of its original members were still alive, including its founder, Lady Eve Balfour, and former president E.F. Schumacher – authors respectively of *The Living Soil* and *Small is Beautiful*, two major works profoundly influential in the organic movement. When Peter joined the Soil Association Council he felt he was its youngest member by almost 40 years, and the traditionalist, older, members strongly disapproved of his anti-nuclear views. Peter felt that they weren't communicating the organic message strongly enough to the public – that the connection between organic farming and the environment wasn't being made sufficiently – and Peter knew it was time for things to change if the movement was to grow. By 1980, two groups of young and inspired organic farmers had formed British Organic Farmers (BOF, headed by Patrick Holden), and the Organic Growers Association (OGA, headed by Peter). A small group of them organized a conference at Cirencester (borrowing £200 from the Soil Association to do so), inviting farmers and growers to attend, and this was really the beginning of the new-wave organic movement of the 1980s which continues with such energy and dedication today. BOF and OGA have now merged together under the Soil Association banner, with Patrick Holden as

Pak choi, an exotic crop grown under cover together with other Chinese vegetables, produced for stir-fry packs for sale in supermarkets.

Yellow peppers and an increasing variety of exotic organic fruits and vegetables are now available because of companies like OFF.

its director, and many of that youthful band of the early eighties remain dedicated members of the council.

For his work, Peter Segger has been awarded the OBE, and in 1999 won the Organic Trophy at the Organic Food Awards, a prize awarded to the individual or company that has made an outstanding contribution to the development of the organic movement in the UK. He is passionately committed to spreading the organic message through education and, although delighted with the support major supermarkets have given the organic movement in making produce more available in the UK, he wants to get them involved with school projects through competitions like 'Young Cook of the Year'. He is convinced that fresh food is the key to good health, and that young people must learn this message early in life.

Lady Eve Balfour called agriculture 'the primary health service', and Peter feels that farmers are not sufficiently respected and valued for their vital role in producing the nation's food. Healthily and naturally produced, it is at the root of our health and, somehow, good-quality fresh food must be made available to all. The National Health Service bears a huge cost for those at the lower end of the income scale, who are not consuming sufficient fresh food, and whose health is suffering as a result. Our health is inherited from the sperm and eggs of our forebears, and so what will happen to future generations if we don't work to improve the health of people today? Peter feels it's unlikely that NHS money would be spent to buy and distribute fresh produce to those in deprived circumstances, so the healthy eating message must spread by education. A huge amount of fresh food is wasted because shops will only sell, or say people will only buy, fruit and veg that is perfect in appearance.

Peter knows that there is much work to be done to spread the message about the value of fresh organic food, and that we must capitalize on the progress made in recent years. When I first met Peter in 1989 at a Soil Association conference dinner, I was charged with telling the story of *The Archers* and the trials and tribulations of early days of organic conversion at Bridge Farm in Ambridge, and presenting spoof awards (in the shape of carrots). I presented Peter Segger with the award for 'Most exaggerated claim'. This claim was to get half of Britain organic by 1992. We all know now that that didn't happen, but if anyone is going to be responsible if it does, Peter Segger is surely going to be one of the prime movers.

practical organics

With imports available, the January shopper can now find supplies of organic fruit and veg in winter. With the inclement weather, January is a time for the grower to get planning. Read up about the basics of organic gardening and decide what crops you'll be planting.

What to try in
january

Vegetables
Baby sweetcorn *(i)*
Beetroot
Broccoli *(i)*
Brussels sprouts
Celery
Chard
Courgettes *(i)*
Jerusalem artichokes
Kale
Kohlrabi
Leeks
Root veg: especially
   celeriac, parsnips,
   swede and turnips
Squash

Fruit
Citrus fruit *(i)*
Grapes *(i)*
Kiwi fruit *(i)*
Lychees *(i)*
Mangoes *(i)*
Melons *(i)*
Pineapples *(i)*

FOR THE SHOPPER

In January, root vegetables still make up the bulk of home-grown produce on offer. Potatoes, carrots, celeriac, parsnips, turnips, swede and Jerusalem artichokes abound, perfect in warming winter soups and stews. Although salad leaves are scarce, many green vegetables, such as Brussels sprouts, leeks and celery, positively thrive after a sharp frost. On the fruit scene there are fewer home-grown options, but there's a range of imports and citrus fruit like oranges, lemons and grapefruit from the Mediterranean are available. (Now's the traditional time to make marmalade.) Towards the end of the month look out for early rhubarb, delicious in old-fashioned crumbles and fools.

Changing the way you eat

Eating the organic way means changing not just the way you cook and eat, but also the way you think about food. We've all got used to abundant produce all year round from all over the world. But we have paid for this apparent variety in terms of taste, flavour and quality. True we can now eat (and indeed expect to be able to eat) strawberries in December and apples in July, but such produce has usually been stored for lengthy periods, transported vast distances and often either artificially ripened or sold in its hard, 'green' state for ripening in the fruit bowl. Its flavour is usually not a patch on a freshly picked, seasonal fruit.

Organic eating means adapting our habits and reverting to eating what nature intended us to eat: buying fresh, local produce in season whenever we can. This means being inspired by what's on offer and seeking out or improvising recipes to use the food available, rather than deciding what you are going to cook and then going in search of the ingredients. Once you get used to it, you'll find it's a much more imaginative way of eating. After all, experimentation is how many of the great recipes of the world came into being.

Organic food is grown without the use of synthetic or artificial chemicals, and fruit and veg are not subject to treatments to enhance their appearance and lengthen shelf-life. Thus, it can sometimes look less appealing and deteriorate more rapidly than its non-organic counterparts, but the benefits to your health, and that of the soil and the environment, more than outweigh these minor disadvantages. And, if you have to eat it up more quickly, this may encourage you to eat more fruit and veg in general, which must be good for you!

Focus: Fruit

The fruit section of the supermarket is an excellent illustration of some of the issues that are causing more and more people to go organic. Indeed, if our great-grandparents were to take a stroll in the fruit section of the average supermarket they would be stunned by the sheer variety of fruits on offer from all parts of the globe – mangoes from India, physalis from Colombia, soursop from the Caribbean to name but a few, nestling alongside the more familiar apples, pears and oranges. However, if they were to look more closely they would also be surprised by the lack of diversity. Apples like Blenheim, Newton's Wonder and Ashmead's Kernel, known and loved by Victorian gardeners, have been replaced by a tide of Golden Delicious, Braeburn and Granny

OFF's distribution centre – checking lemons to ensure they meet the highest quality standards.

are some of those foods most likely to have been exposed to high levels of chemicals, such as artificial fertilizers and pesticides and post-harvest chemicals. Although these may ensure that fruit looks healthy and appetizing, because fruit loses nutrients such as vitamin C while it is stored that shiny, red apple may actually contain fewer vitamins by the time you eat it.

Uniformity

Fruits ripen at different times and come in a variety of shapes and sizes. Conventional EU classifications demand that fruit is uniform in shape and size, and blemish free. Uniformity may make fruit easier to pack, store and trans-port but it means using more chemicals to produce its uniformity. It also means that plant varieties are bred specifically for uniformity, rather than individuality. Much research is being done about the possibility of genetically modify-ing fruit (see p 85), to enhance flavour and resistance to disease, slow the ripening process, and reduce oxidation/browning when cut.

Smith's usually imported from places like New Zealand and North America. With pears, old varieties like Beurre Hardy have been abandoned in favour of the all-pervasive Williams, Comice and Conference.

Over the past 30 years, the UK has lost half its pear and over 60% of its apple orchards. Part of the reason for this, and for the consequent lack of diversity, is due to the requirements of supply-ing fruit for a mass market. Because fruit is bought and distributed from central depots it's hard, if not impossible, to get local, seasonal produce. The UK's disappearing apple and pear orchards are a matter of concern because they are, especially if organically managed, home to a wide variety of wildlife, insects and birds.

Although there is undoubtedly more fruit available to the shopper now, quality often leaves a lot to be desired. Conventionally grown fruits

Poisoned apple?

In 1996 an average Cox's apple tree could have been sprayed 16 times with 36 different pesticide ingredients. Apples near the inside of the tree are unlikely to receive as much spray as apples nearer the outside. Research carrried out by the UK Pesticides Safety Directorate, which tests food for pesticides, has found that pesticide residues vary tremendously even for apples in the same batch. For instance, a 'hot' apple could contain 13 times as much pesticide as another apple in the same testing batch.
Source: Pesticides News, March 1999

Feeling fruity? The facts about fruit

Apples and pears: Apples are some of the fruits most heavily exposed to chemicals. In 1998 residues were detected in 69% of dessert apples and 96% of pears sampled by the UK's Working Party on Pesticide Residues (WPPR). By buying organic apples and pears, especially locally through box schemes or from the farm gate, you are not only avoiding exposure to potentially harmful pesticides you are also encouraging farmers to grow organic – and to grow more varieties, especially those that are naturally hardy and resistant to diseases such as scab.

Bananas: Organic bananas are becoming more readily available mainly because of publicity about the non-organic kinds that have frequently been sprayed with large amounts of chemicals, hazardous to plantation workers and the consumer.

Citrus fruit: Those tempting non-organic oranges wouldn't be so alluring if you knew they contained pesticide residues, that their bright orange colour is artificial and that their shiny skin is due to wax, applied to prevent it going mouldy. In 1998 multiple pesticide residues were found in 62 of 66 samples analysed by the WPPR, though none exceeded the recommended limits. By buying organic, you are ensuring that your oranges and lemons are free of such chemicals. Organic citrus fruit does go off more quickly, so store it in the fridge and use it up quickly – you'll benefit as the fresher your fruit the more nutrients it retains.

Exotic fruit: Globalization of food production is responsible for much of the loss of diversity in food, as crops may be grown for their ability to travel and stay fresh, rather than their taste and individuality. Organic exotic fruits have also been transported vast distances and this does raise the question about nutrition levels. But buying organic will mean that you don't get the chemicals and that you are supporting a whole philosophy about sustainable, eco-friendly agriculture as well as encouraging cultural and social development for the local producers, who are encouraged not to sell more than 50% of their produce to protect themselves from potential collapses in the changeable export markets. Valuable fossil fuels are used up to transport produce, so although exotic fruit adds variety to your fruit basket, try to buy locally grown, too, and support diversity in the market.

Peaches, nectarines and soft fruit: These are especially susceptible to fungal diseases and non-organic varieties are sprayed to avoid this. In 1998 pesticide residues were detected in 54% of 72 samples of peaches and nectarines analysed, and multiple residues were found in 18% (though none exceeded maximum recommended limits). Organically grown soft fruit is still in quite short supply, but some box schemes and farm shops sell it. Better still, grow your own!

Pesticide problems

One of the biggest worries about fruit is the use of pesticides and post-harvest chemicals: fungicides and waxes designed to prevent fruit looking wrinkled and unappetizing and to prolong shelf-life. Unlike chemicals applied during growth, post-harvest chemicals are designed to adhere and are difficult to wash off. The result being that we consume them.

Among the chemicals causing concern are organophospates (OPs for short), a group of pesticides used on apples, bananas and soft fruits, as well as many vegetables, which affect the nervous system. This is a problem not only for consumers but also for agricultural workers, especially in developing countries, where large amounts of these chemicals are often used. Symptoms associated with OP exposure can include headaches, sweating, breathing problems, blurred vision, nausea, loss of memory and even death. The UK Pesticides Network is pressing for OPs to be banned, but, in the meantime, your only means to be sure of avoiding them – and of doing your bit for the world – is to grow or buy organic.

Other chemicals causing concern are the endocrine-disrupting chemicals, that disturb the body's hormonal system. These include insecticides and fungicides that may have been used on beans, peas, apple blossom, kiwi fruit, peaches, nectarines, tomatoes and wine grapes, and soft fruits such as plums and blackcurrants, among others.

As well as their effects on humans, there is also the issue of the effects of some agrichemicals on the environment. For example, some fungicides used on raspberries and strawberries, deplete ozone.

Although the government monitors pesticide residues for safety, and there is no

Produce, like these cherry tomatoes from Holland, arrives in bulk from organic producers and is re-packed and distributed throughout the UK.

suggestion that they are at danger levels, what nobody knows for certain is what the continual effect of ingesting small amounts of different pesticide residues over a period of time, the so-called 'cocktail effect', is. It is of particular concern for babies and small children, pregnant and breastfeeding women and older people whose bodies are less able to resist adverse effects.

In a recent survey, for example, three-fifths of apples tested contained residues and, although these were well below those allowed by law, it's interesting to learn that the government recommends peeling apples before eating them to avoid pesticide residues, even though the highest levels of nutrients are found just beneath the apple skin. There's also an issue surrounding pesticide use in developing countries – the rules about the use here of chemicals that are banned in the UK are less strict. These chemicals are sold in the developing world, thus leading to what's known as the 'toxic boomerang' effect whereby they find their way into our food here, regardless of our rules.

FOR THE GROWER

More and more people are beginning to garden organically. Nothing can beat the pleasure of being able to pop out to pick a fresh, crisp lettuce, sweet ripe tomatoes and a few herbs for an impromptu summer salad. Everyone can find the space for a few vegetables, even those with only a small garden or plot. Even if you live in a flat in a town, you can still grow your own produce: for example, herbs can be grown in a window box, tomatoes can be grown in hanging baskets and peas and beans look attractive in a large decorative pot, twining up peasticks.

Focus: Growing organically

Growing organically is not just a question of using green manures instead of chemical fertilizers. It means thinking about gardening in a new, more 'holistic', way. Instead of zapping every insect and weed you see, you need to learn to welcome nature's diversity and positively encourage birds and insects and other wildlife, recognizing that some can be a help in keeping pests at bay and your garden healthy. You need to understand that it's no good growing vegetables organically if you continue to use artificial fertilizers and pesticides elsewhere in the garden, for example, on the lawn or in the flower bed. The organic garden is a whole environment and any artificial chemicals you use will seep into the earth and be taken up by your organic crops.

At this time of year when it's usually bitterly cold there is little you can do in the garden except try to minimize the worst effects of the weather. In the meantime you can dream about summer and plan your planting. If you've never grown vegetables before, think about where in your garden you want to put your vegetable plot.

Throughout this book you'll find a host of tips to remind you what to do, and when, if you are new to organic gardening. There are plenty of excellent books now on the market to give you detailed advice and help you get started (see p 190).

Garden jobs for January

- Clean and sort any seeds you or a friend have saved from last year, putting them in packets and labelling them, ready for use. Keep in a cool, dark dry place
- Sow carrots, radishes, peas, broad beans, spinach and parsley under light cover
- Sow onions and cover with straw
- Plant garlic and horseradish
- Pot up mint roots to bring in for the windowsill
- Sow tomatoes under glass
- Cover rhubarb and sea kale for forcing

- Prune apples, pears, gooseberries and currant bushes
- Cut back newly planted blackcurrants and blackberries and hybrid berries and raspberries to give them the opportunity to grow strong roots
- Fork around existing canes to expose over-wintering pests to birds
- Plant fruit trees and bushes
- Check greasebands (see p 39)
- Hang fat up in trees to attract insect-eating birds
- Hoe lightly around fruit trees to expose pests to birds

Plan your planting and buy your seeds now – endive lettuce will add variety to your summer salads.

TIP: SOURCING SEEDS

Settle down with a few seed catalogues and plan your summer growing. Organic seeds are getting easier to find, but if you can't get them from your usual supplier or garden centre try the HDRA's *Organic Gardening Catalogue* or the French seed company Terre de Semences (see p 190). If a friend already gardens organically, ask them for spare seeds from last year's crops – don't forget to save your own seeds each year, once you get started.

Organic gardening means:

• Working with, rather than subduing, nature
• Building soil fertility for healthier crops, rather than applying artificial fertilizers
• Minimizing pollution and damage to the whole environment
• Avoiding artificial chemicals: no chemical fertilizers, fungicides or pesticides and keeping pests at bay using natural methods
• Protecting and enhancing the whole garden environment and its genetic diversity, including protecting wild plants and wildlife habitats

---

Rhubarb and ginger galette

A deliciously warming winter tart.

Preparation time: 15 minutes
Cooking time: 20 minutes
Serves: 4

50 g organic butter, softened
50 g organic caster sugar
1 large organic egg yolk
1 tbsp cornflour
50 g ground organic almonds
2 pieces stem ginger,
    very finely chopped
1 tbsp stem ginger syrup
250 g puff pastry
225 g organic rhubarb, sliced diagonally into
    2–3-cm pieces
1 tbsp icing sugar, plus extra to dust

1. Preheat the oven to 220C/425F/Gas 7. In a large bowl cream the butter and sugar together. Beat in the egg yolk. Fold in the cornflour, ground almonds, stem ginger and syrup. Chill.
2. Roll the pastry out on a lightly floured surface to a 26-cm square and cut out four 12-cm circles. Using a sharp knife, held horizontally against the edge of the pastry, knock up against the cut sides (marking the flakes, or layers, like this helps them separate successfully as the pastry rises). Flute the edges by pressing the back of the knife vertically around the edges at intervals. Arrange the circles, evenly spaced, on a baking sheet.
3. Divide the ginger and ground almond mixture between the pastry circles and spread out, leaving a 1.5-cm border clear. Arrange the rhubarb over the top. Sift over the icing sugar. Bake for 15–20 minutes until golden and slightly scorched.
4. Lightly dust with extra icing sugar. serve immediately with vanilla ice-cream or crème fraîche.

february

Rachel Rowlands began making yogurt at her organic farm, Brynllys, on the west coast of Wales in 1984. Today Rachel's Organic Dairy products are a household name, on supermarket shelves throughout the UK, as well as in independent retailers and health food shops.

The business, which has its base on a trading estate in Aberystwyth, was taken over by the American company Horizon Organic Dairy in April 1999 in a multi-million-pound deal. Sales continue to grow and huge expansion projects are planned. Pat Archer's organic dairy and yogurt-making business has been a vital element in *The Archers'* organic story of Bridge Farm, Ambridge. If one were to mix fact with fiction it would surely be that Pat would look with huge admiration and inspiration at her fellow country-woman Rachel Rowlands. Pat's yogurt sells well, but not in that league. Maybe her new Borchester shop will help increase her sales!

I'd seen how the Rachel's brand had taken off in the supermarkets, had heard and read much of the story of the woman behind it, and wanted very much to meet her for myself. (My colleague Colin Skipp [Tony Archer] had visited Rachel's Dairy in 1988, but there have been many changes made since then.) So one bright, sunny winter Saturday I visited Rachel and Gareth.

The 250-acre Brynllys Farm was bought by Rachel's grandmother in 1942, at a time when all farms were in fact organic, although the term wasn't then used. It was the shortage of food caused by the Second World War that led to the change from traditional farming methods to the use of artificial fertilizers and pesticides, in an effort to increase food production. Both Rachel's grandmother and mother were strong believers in good nutrition and health, and in natural methods of food production. At the age of 18 Rachel's mother, Dinah Williams, had been ill and was cured by nature cure practitioners using natural means. She adhered to a strict diet, and believed in the power of nature to heal, and now, at the age of 88, Dinah is a healthy and still-active family member on the farm. 'She last had medical attention 50 years ago when my sister was born,' Rachel told me, and when I met her she was energetically pushing a wheelbarrow, on her way to check up on a sick cow. She believes that one of the secrets to her long life and good health is her daily afternoon nap!

It was a chance meeting between Rachel's parents, and the inspirational founder of the Soil Association, Lady Eve Balfour, that convinced them that farming organically was the right approach, and fertilizers and pesticides have never been used at Brynllys. When Rachel and Gareth took over the running of the farm from Rachel's parents in 1966, they continued the organic tradition. Throughout the sixties and seventies many ridiculed them for their beliefs, but they stuck to their principles and beliefs in organics. Organic farming, they both agreed, gave them a wonderful quality of life, even if it meant doing things like having to keep their tractor for five

Rachel's original yogurt-making equipment.

instead of three years. They were happy raising their family, who began to take an interest and became involved with the farm's running, too, and as Gareth pointed out, 'Why complicate things and go looking for problems.'

It is amazing to think that if the exceptionally bad winter of 1982 hadn't occurred, the story of Rachel's Organic Dairy might never have happened. The farm was cut off by huge snowfalls and for 10 days the milk tanker couldn't get through to collect their milk. Rachel refused to waste the milk and she resurrected old separating equipment to separate the milk and produce cream, which she sold locally. It proved popular, and shops and hotels wanted more. With good, friendly local contacts the farm took the rather unusual step of offering their cream on a sale or return basis. Any that did come back was made into butter, and the buttermilk and skimmed milk left over from the original cream-making was fed to the cattle and pigs. Surplus was frozen and nothing was wasted. That winter must have been really hard for Rachel as Gareth broke his leg in a fall, trying to get a digger out to clear a path through the snows, and was hospitalized for several weeks. Rachel had to run the farm without his help, but the harshness of the winter had given birth to a great business.

Selling through their local contacts had proved so successful, they decided to branch out into bigger product ranges. There were marketing opportunities in selling more than one item to the same shop and so, in 1984, Rachel experimented with making yogurt, on the Aga in the farmhouse kitchen, using left-over skimmed milk from the cream. She eventually found a recipe that worked well, and still today her yogurt is made only from purest ingredients, with no stabilizers, preservatives, sweeteners or powders. The timing was fortuitous as attitudes were beginning to change and people were becoming more concerned about how their food was produced. Rachel and Gareth are sure that if they had started the dairy business 10 years earlier it would not have succeeded, but their business grew in the receptive and enthusiastic market of the eighties, and they increased their product range to 12 items, including cottage cheese as well as the yogurt, butter and cream.

An old butter churn, used in the first days of the dairy. These old pieces of equipment can be seen in Rachel's interpretive centre (the old calving building) where school groups and others can come to learn about organic farming.

The distinctive black and white labels used on Rachel's produce have led to a huge boost in sales since they were introduced in 1998.

By 1985 the name Rachel's had been chosen to brand the products, and the old farm buildings were developed into a dairy production area. Continually testing the market, Rachel and Gareth knew they needed a corporate image, and in 1986 a logo was designed for the pots. By 1987 they opened the farm to the public, offering guided farm walks, and created a farm shop. The market for the dairy products was expanding way beyond west Wales and in 1989 they undertook a feasibility study on the future of the dairy. The outcome of the study basically came down to whether they could continue running the business on the farm, or move to other premises. The decision to relocate was taken, a large loan taken out and, in May 1992, the business moved to a bespoke dairy unit on the Glanyrafon Industrial Estate outside Aberystwyth. 'Business was the name of the game,' says Gareth, 'we needed total commitment to make it work'; and by dividing their talents – Rachel took charge of the processing floor, and Gareth managed personnel and finance, with the farm itself now, inevitably, taking something of a back seat – they worked hard to add to their success. It took a further three years to make the business really work, but the organic message got through, and they got their big breakthrough as their produce found its way into the supermarkets.

In 1996 further expansion and borrowing took place, and Rachel's Organic Dairy started to make decent money. Rachel and Gareth, who had never drawn salaries from the business, managed to do so for the first time. They'd never been afraid to seek expert advice during the time that they were building the business, and they firmly believed in investing in promotion. Although they couldn't really afford to do so at the time, they hired a PR company. They also changed their accountants to the multinational Coopers and Lybrand, and in 1997 engaged design consultants to look to the future of the marketing. After considering several packaging options, they eventually settled for the distinctive black and white pots we recognize in the shops today. They come from Denmark, are made from one material, have tamper-proof resealable lids, and are recyclable. Discovered by the company's Operation's Manager, Gareth and Rachel's son John, they have led to a tremendous boost in sales since they were introduced in 1998, and taking the unusual step of using black in the packaging of dairy products has paid off. In July 1998 HRH The Prince of Wales officially opened the phase 2 extension to Rachel's Organic Dairy in Aberystwyth.

On 1 April 1999 Rachel's Dairy was bought by America's top organic milk company, Horizon Organic Dairy. Horizon, America's biggest organic dairy supplier with over 60% of the home market, was founded in 1992 in Colorado by two health food specialists and supports US farming co-operatives and other organic producers. Their mission statement says, 'Horizon Organic Dairy produces and sells quality organic milk products of good value to consumers who are concerned about food safety, the environment, animal welfare, and health and nutrition for themselves and their families.'

They are pledged to big expansion plans for the Aberystwyth dairy, and plan to expand the organic market throughout the UK. Rachel and Gareth remain crucially involved with the company as specialist consultants, and foresee an exciting future for both organics and Wales. Extra promotion and marketing will increase the demand for organic milk, thus encouraging more farmers to convert to organic farming methods. And as Rachel recently said in a talk to Milk Marque farmers: 'The success of the new company offers real benefits to farmers and the rural economy. Rachel's Organic Dairy will be strengthened by Horizon's investment, thus protecting and increasing the number of jobs in rural Wales.' The deal has also secured for the Rowlands the future of Brynllys Farm for future generations.

When the dairy business took off the farm shop closed, but the farm still welcomes visitors by arrangement. The old calving building now serves as an interpretive centre where school groups and others can learn about organic farming. I noticed boxes of empty yogurt pots and Rachel explained the scheme she operates with schools, whereby groups are paid to collect the pots, which are then recycled into energy. Experiments are being carried out to investigate the possibility of turning them into garden furniture, too!

The walk up the hill behind the farmhouse leads to a ridge which has stunning views across the estuary of the River Dovey to the seaside town of Aberdovey in one direction, and the mountains in the other. There are natural springs all over the farm, and Rachel's son has piped water from them

Making yogurt at the dairy in Aberystwyth.

across the hill for irrigation. The land is quite marshy in places, and there is an area of reclaimed bog, Borth Bog, which is purported to be the oldest raised bog in the country. The bogland is very fertile as the peat holds water and nutrients, and the banks have pockets of gorse, which, when it was necessary in exceptionally severe winter conditions, her grand-mother fed to animals.

During my visit to the farm, the cattle were in for the winter. Rachel explained that too many animals grazing on the fields in winter ploughs up the land and destroys the pasture, especially in wet conditions. Sheep were still grazing outside, but due to come in any day as lambing was about to begin.

There are around 200 livestock on the farm, which has a milking herd of 60 and a smaller beef herd. They have a magnificent MRI (Meuse, Rhine, Issel) beef bull, who also breeds to a percentage of the dairy herd. They have crossed a Fresian bull to some of the Guernsey cows, but Rachel is going back more towards pure-bred Guernseys again. There were animals at various stages in the farm buildings, including young stock and cows with calves feeding on their mothers' milk, and there was a beautifully contented feeling to the place. It's clear that Rachel loves and respects her animals. 'Livestock must be well managed,' she says, 'we have to respect animals and not just use them for our own convenience.' She is a successful businesswoman but still very much a farmer at heart, and involved with the welfare of her stock. She discusses breeding plans with her stockman, knows her cows individually, and she loves to wander through the cowsheds at night, listening to them. I had commented on the contented sound of chewing, and Rachel explained that at night you can hear it even more clearly, and in the relative quiet of late evening she can quickly pick up sounds of an animal in distress.

I went on to pay a visit to the dairy premises in Aberystwyth, and even on a Saturday afternoon it was busy as they work a seven-day week. We put on white coats, hats and overshoes, and scrubbed up before entering the hi-tech food processing area. Rachel showed me the huge separator tanks, and the inoculating tanks where milk goes after separating and before it is fed into machines for either pot set or bulk set yogurt. As it was getting towards late afternoon, production had stopped for the day and much scrubbing of equipment and hosing down of floors was taking place: health regulations

are very strict. Work was to begin again on Sunday morning, when the plain yogurt produced that Saturday would be turned into fruit yogurt. The dairy produce all their own conserves from fruit that is hand washed – very time consuming – and they would like to find a company to produce these for them, but so far no one has been able to get the flavour right, and they will not sacrifice their high standards.

Cows going out into the fields for the first time later in spring – a day the cows and the farmers always look forward to.

There were pallets of yogurt ready for despatch, and in addition to using their own lorries they have also done a delivery deal with Safeway. The Safeway lorry makes its final drop at its Aberystwyth supermarket, before returning to the central despatch depot in Warrington. As Rachel's products are also despatched from Warrington, the lorry now makes its homeward run full of Rachel's Dairy produce and this has enabled the dairy to take one of its lorries off the road. It is a practical and environmentally friendly deal which has also saved the company a lot of money.

In the office, Rachel showed me the plans that have been drawn up to expand the existing factory building into the neighbouring field. The extension will be massive. They were then processing 4–5 million litres of milk per year and this is set to rise to 50 million. The dairy currently has a

Rachel feeding a lamb. Although a very successful business-woman, she remains a farmer at heart with a deep love and respect for her animals.

staff of 54, but many more jobs will obviously be created. Rachel's Organic Dairy, as part of its commitment to organic farming, is to launch a series of three-year student bursaries at the University of Wales in Aberystwyth. The bursaries will be used to promote the University's Welsh Institute of Rural Studies and it is hoped that high-calibre students, who will develop interests in organic agriculture, will be attracted.

There have been many changes at Rachel's Dairy since those early days of yogurt-making experiments on the Aga and deliveries in a van lined with duvets for temperature control. The future for the organic market looks set for further and greater success under the Horizon deal and Rachel remains totally committed to her beliefs in organic farming. In 1996 she was awarded the MBE for her work and she frequently speaks to farming and other audiences. Recently she took as her theme the writings of Lady Eve Balfour who in her book *The Living Soil* said, 'Close contact with nature effectively counteracts any tendency to overrate the achievements of man. To cultivate health, one must first cultivate a vital environment. Health is a mutual synthesis of organism and environment. Unless both man and his environment are obeying the biological law of mutual synthesis, there can be no health.' Rachel is convinced that those words are as relevant today as when they were written in 1943. Lady Eve's inspirational work is the very essence of the beliefs of Rachel and of all organic farmers.

practical organics

Despite the sharpness of the weather, the snowdrops and other spring bulbs are in bloom and there's a hint of spring in the air. In the kitchen it's still a time for rib-sticking meals, but you can easily work them off in the garden by digging in preparation for spring sowing.

What to try in
february

Vegetables
Broccoli *(i)*
Brussels sprouts
Cabbage
Celery *(i)*
Chicory
Courgettes *(i)*
Ginger *(i)*
Jerusalem artichokes
Leeks
Salsify
Spring Greens
Squash
Root veg: especially
　winter radishes

Fruit
Avocados *(i)*
Bananas *(i)*
Cherries *(i)*
Grapes *(i)*
Lemons *(i)*
Mangoes *(i)*
Pineapples *(i)*
Rhubarb

FOR THE SHOPPER

There are various ways to buy organic produce: supermarkets, box schemes, farmers' markets and farm shops. The April chapter goes into these in detail (see pp 67–8), as spring is when produce really starts to become abundant. Many box schemes run down during winter when salads and fruit are in shorter supply. Some may close down completely, and others may provide a bag or box of root veg and some seasonal greens on a monthly rather than a weekly basis at this time of year. But, there are lots of root vegetables around and, with a little imagination, there are endless ways to cook and serve them (see below and p 39).

In the shops there are few salad leaves around at the moment and often those that are can be flabby and tend to be rather tasteless and listless because they aren't grown outside. Harsh weather and lack of sunlight during the winter months mean that lettuces have to be grown in greenhouses or under cover and are slow to mature and more prone to disease. To combat this they are sprayed repeatedly with pesticides. In fact according to SUSTAIN, the National Food Alliance, the average non-organic lettuce – winter or summer – has 11 doses of pesticide during its short life. Not surprising then that the 1998 report of the UK's Working Party on Pesticide Residues found residues in 84% of samples tested and multiple residues in 72%. More worryingly still, some of these exceeded the recommended limit for pesticide residues.

A good reason then to eat seasonally and snap up the range of robust winter greens that positively thrive in cold conditions – organic leeks, broccoli, spring greens and loads of different cabbages are flourishing this month. Not watery, school-dinner, boiled cabbage but finely shredded and briefly stir-fried to bring out the flavour and crunchy texture. Or cook it long and slow in a casserole until it is meltingly soft and tasty. Serve cabbage in small, tasteful portions to complement a hearty stew or casserole. Try glazed white cabbage, casseroled red cabbage with apple, or deep blue-black Italian cavolo nero – a natural partner for borlotti beans or pasta.

It's a lean month for native fruit but imported lemons, bananas and mangoes are all available now.

Focus: Yogurt, cheese and dairy produce

The quality of any kind of dairy produce – be it cheese, yogurt, butter or whatever – lies fundamentally in the quality of the milk. The best

---

TIP: VEGETABLE DELIGHTS

How about baby turnips boiled and tossed in orange butter, or swedes mashed with butter and pepper? Root veg also make an excellent base for soups and stews. Roasted root veg soups are popular in trendy restaurants now as their naturally sweet, earthy flavours are enhanced by roasting and complemented by the aromatic taste of herbs. Such soups are easy to re-create for yourself at home – simply roast the roots, perhaps with an onion and some cloves of garlic, then blend with a good homemade stock. Add a few herbs, *et voilà*! Try roast Jerusalem artichoke soup with rosemary, roast carrots and parsnips with thyme, roast potato soup with garlic, or roast squash and rosemary.

yogurt, cheese and butter undoubtedly come from organic milk taken from cows that have been reared with concern for their welfare and health, grazed in organic pastures with healthy soil and winter-fed on organic feed. The March chapter deals with the details of organic milk production (see p 50).

Yogurt

The flavour and nutritional quality of a good organic yogurt is incomparable. The quality depends on two factors: the milk it's made from and the culturing process that turns it into yogurt.

Most modern, commercial yogurts – and unfortunately this includes many organic ones, although not Rachel's – are made with dried rather than fresh milk. The drying process destroys the natural balance of fats, sugars and protein in the milk – and hence the yogurt. In a fresh-milk yogurt the bacteria (added to convert milk to yogurt) feed on the milk sugar (lactose) and set the proteins to create a smooth, delicious yogurt in which the sweetness is delicately balanced against sourness. It also has a very low lactose content, which makes it easily digested, especially by those with a lactose intolerance. Dried-milk yogurt has a higher lactose content and is thus more indigestible.

How organic is organic yogurt?

Because of the demands of commercial production, bacterial culture has to be bought in the form of freeze-dried pellets. At the time of writing these are not yet guaranteed to be grown on an organic culture medium. Regulations governing organic food stipulate that they may contain up to 5% non-organic ingredients, so the freeze-dried non-organic pellets fall within the organic remit. With the increasing demand for organic food, however, it seems likely that the manufacturers will bow to pressure to produce an organic culture medium in the not too distant future.

Some organic fruit yogurts may contain a variety of permitted non-organic additives, such as pectin (used as a thickener) and stabilizers, though nowhere near the number found in non-organic yogurts. The simplest yogurt is generally the best.

Always check the ingredients list. If the yogurt is made with fresh milk, it should have no more than 4% protein and 3.3–3.8% fat (10% in Greek yogurt). If the fat content is 4% or above, it is almost certainly made with dried milk. Carbohydrate content should be maximum 5% in a plain or 10% in a fruit yogurt. The fewer ingredients it has the better.

Despite their healthy image, most commercially produced, non-organic yogurts (especially flavoured ones) are highly processed products which contain a whole host of additives, flavourings, thickeners and so on. In peasant societies where yogurt was traditionally made it was produced simply from the action of a bacterium, *bifidus bulgaris*, in milk with nothing added or taken away. A small amount of each batch of yogurt was kept behind and added to the next bowl of milk to produce more yogurt.

Bifidus bulgaris produces a thinnish, quite sour yogurt that is not to our more sophisticated taste nowadays. For this reason most commercial yogurts today are made with four different bacteria designed to temper the sourness slightly and produce the thicker, firmer-textured yogurt preferred by today's consumers. These are *lactobacillus bulgaris, streptococcus thermophilus, bifidus bifida* and *lactobacillus acidophilus.* The latter two occur naturally in the human gut and help boost the immune system. In a 'live' yogurt the bacteria continue to work in the gut to keep a healthy balance of gut bacteria which, in turn, helps stimulate the action of the immune system. However, in most standard, non-organic yogurts the bacteria are treated so they stop working and have no health benefits. Sadly even many so-called 'live' yogurts do not contain enough live culture to make a difference to you.

The challenge of producing a well-flavoured, creamy yogurt that is neither too sour nor too sweet, too thick nor too thin, lies in maintaining the natural balance between all the different ingredients. According to Rachel Rowlands, too much *streptococcus* and too little *bulgaris* and *acidophilus* and you end up with a distinctly unappetizing gooey mess.

Once you've tasted organic cheese you won't want to go back to eating the bland, rubbery variety.

Cheese

A growing range of organic cheeses is now available, both home produced and imported. The best and most flavoursome are undoubtedly those made by small, independent cheesemakers from their own organically reared cows. These are usually not available in supermarkets. You can get them from specialist cheese or organic shops, at the farm gate and farmers' markets. However, cheeses made on a commercial scale – using organic milk from several farms and sold mainly through supermarkets – are still a tremendous improvement on the bland, rubbery stuff that so often passes for cheese in our shops.

Organic cheese is full of flavour and is guaranteed to be free of artificial flavourings and colourings (although annatto is allowed for traditional English coloured cheeses like Red Leicester) and has no added vitamins or minerals. Where no organic ingredient is available, up to 5% of non-organic food ingredients are permitted. However, if non-organic synthetic coatings are used on the cheese, this must be declared on the label.

Like yogurt, the quality of cheese depends crucially on the milk from which it is made. The key, as so often, lies in the superior attention to detail that goes into organic farming methods. In conventional farming cows are fed on one type of grass or feed. Organic cows are fed a varied diet which is influenced by the region of the country they are bred in, the types of grasses they graze on and the soil the grass grows on. Rachel Rowlands says that when she used to make her own farm cheeses buyers could distinguish when the cows had been moved to a different pasture simply from the taste of the cheese. Cheese connoisseurs agree that the tastiest, most flavoursome cheese is made from milk produced during the spring when the cows are eating fresh grass, so try out a cheese from a small independent organic cheesemaker sold between August to Christmas to taste the difference.

Another factor to be aware of is that non-organic cheese, especially if produced on a large commercial scale, may have been made with a genetically engineered enzyme called chymosin, a form of rennet.

Butter

The diet of the cow again plays an important role in the flavour of butter, which is why organic butter is more flavoursome.

Butter is often seen as unhealthy and high in saturated fat, which clogs arteries and leads to heart disease. Not surprising then that many of us now opt to eat margarine instead. In fact, despite its image as a healthy spread, margarine is a totally manufactured food, full of artificial additives, flavourings and colourings.

The tide of opinion is changing, however, with the discovery that some margarines are a source of trans-fatty acids, which some experts believe to be as harmful as saturated animal fat. Consuming small quantities of wholesome butter, which has not been over-processed and interfered with, must be better than eating large quantities of an artificial product. It's a myth that all butter is full of unhealthy saturated fats. The diet of the cow produces variations, according to Rachel Rowlands, with cows fed on wheat producing a hard butter, high in saturated fats. Cows fed on oats produce a softer, healthier butter. As farmers have been given subsidies to grow wheat, few butters, even organic ones, come from cows fed oats. However, it is yet another example of the connection between farming practices and the food we eat. Living the organic way means becoming aware of these connections and making your food choices accordingly.

Pasture-fed, organically reared cows produce healthy milk to make tastier butter.

FOR THE GROWER

The weather is likely to determine how much time you can spend in the garden this month but, if there are some mild days, it's an ideal opportunity to dig over your vegetable plot and prepare for spring planting. Spend some time reading and planning and get acquainted with what's in store for creating an organic garden. If you haven't chosen your seeds yet, you should do so now. Once you have all your packets, lay them out in groups according to where you are going to plant them (see crop rotation information p 86, to help in planning your veg plot).

Focus: Enriching your soil

The fertility of your soil is the foundation on which everything you grow depends. The best way to enhance soil quality is to add organic matter – that's rotted down, living material such as leaves, grass or other vegetation, which helps hold water and nutrients and supplies the soil with food. You should aim to return all waste matter to your soil – if you want to be purist, use only the peelings from organic fruit and vegetables – and supplement it with additional organic (where possible) manure or a soil conditioner.

Garden jobs for February

- Dig in green manures where you can
- Sow mustard and winter tares for green manure (see p 70)
- Dig out perennial weeds
- Sow broad beans, onions, peas, lettuce, cabbage, parsnips, radishes and spring onions in mild, less exposed areas
- Transplant overwintered cos lettuce to final position
- Prune peaches, apricots, nectarines and figs
- Plant fruit trees and bushes
- Check greasebands and renew grease if necessary
- Net fruit trees and bushes if you spot bullfinches pecking off developing flowers and fruit
- Prune out cankered branches of fruit trees and bushes and destroy
- If you are lucky enough to have a large, heated greenhouse, start melons and kidneys beans off there

Trefoil, a green manure, grown to enrich the soil.

Manure is the best soil conditioner (more detail in April chapter p 70) but you should also include kitchen waste, lawn mowings, hedge clippings and vegetable waste from the garden. Ideally as much of this as possible should be organic, but in the real world this is not always possible, so do what you can and treat everything in an organic manner once it passes your garden gate.

There are also a number of organic soil conditioners, available in sacks or growbags, from garden centres and catalogues such as that produced by the HDRA. These include cocoa shell, composted bark, coir fibre and a number of other organic materials such as mushroom

Greasebands

A greaseband is, as the name suggests, a band of grease that is applied around the trunk of fruit trees. This prevents ants, earwigs and other insects from climbing up the tree to lay their eggs. Buy them from garden centres or try Chase Organic's *Organic Gardening Catalogue* (see the Useful Addresses list on p 190).

compost and seaweed. It's also worth seeking out organic waste from local factories, such as spent hops, wool shoddy, vegetable matter and fruit pulps, if you have any in the vicinity.

Celeriac and blue cheese soup

This wonderful soup is a winter-warmer classic. Serve it with some deep-fried sage leaves and crusty organic bread for a hearty start to a February supper or as a meal in itself.

Preparation time: 10 minutes
Cooking time: 25 minutes
Serves: 4

25 g organic butter
1 medium organic onion, chopped
750 g organic celeriac, peeled and cut into
  2-cm chunks
1 large organic baking potato, chopped
2 tbsp roughly chopped fresh organic
  sage leaves
600 ml organic vegetable stock
300 ml organic single cream
200 g organic blue cheese such as Stilton or
  dolcelatte, diced
Seasoning
Fresh organic chives, to garnish
Deep-fried organic sage leaves, to garnish

1. Melt the butter in a large pan and gently fry the vegetables and sage for 5 minutes. Stir in the stock and bring to the boil. Cover the pan and simmer for 15 minutes until the vegetables are tender.
2. Transfer to a food processor and process until smooth (you may need to do this in several batches).
3. Return the soup to the pan and stir in the single cream and half the blue cheese. Cook over a low heat until the cheese has melted, but do not allow to boil. Season to taste.
4. Divide the soup between serving bowls and sprinkle with remaining blue cheese, chives and deep-fried sage leaves to serve.

To make deep-fried sage leaves: heat some oil in a pan and test heat by dropping in a piece of bread – it should turn golden in 1 minute. Add the sage leaves and fry for about 1 minute until crisp and darkened. Because of the high water content, they may spit, so be careful. Drain on kitchen paper.

march

Pimhill Farm stands high on Harmer Hill, near Shrewsbury, with magnificent views stretching across the Shropshire Plain. A working farm growing wheat, oats and vegetables, with a herd of 175 Holstein milking cows and 15 Jerseys, it has been organic since 1949.

Its present owner, Ginny Mayall, is the third generation of her family to run the farm. I first met her when she asked me to open her farm shop in 1998, and meeting the Mayall family and visiting their glorious farm had been a real treat, so I needed no persuasion to keep a promise made to return.

The day I made my return visit the weather looked threatening but, as I got closer to Pimhill, the rain began to clear. I was looking forward to walking Ginny's farm trail – part of the Soil Association Farm Demonstration Network. Pimhill is the first farm to join this scheme, which aims to demonstrate organic farming in practice so that people can gain a greater understanding of its principles.

The trail is a relatively new addition to Pimhill, but the farm shop and the farmyard itself, with piglets, lambs, goats and Muscovy ducks, have proved popular attractions for many years. Blossom the shire horse and her devoted companion, Jenny the donkey, are firm favourites, too. Ginny believes that her customers, some of whom travel many miles to buy organic produce, should have an enjoyable and rewarding experience when they come to Pimhill and has set out to create an attractive and welcoming atmosphere. As she says, 'Farms generally have what other people going into business are clamouring for – space – and we have space… in a lovely setting, with wonderful views.'

Part of the beautiful farm trail through Rabbit Hill Wood, planted in 1966.

The first farm shop opened here in 1988, mainly to sell Pimhill's home-grown and milled flour, and a range of organically produced meat and vegetables. The tiny premises meant that Ginny wasn't able to offer the quality of service and range of produce that she felt her customers wanted and, with the demand for organic produce growing, she took the bold step of making a big investment and expanded the shop to four times its original size, creating an organic café at the same time. Ginny's husband, architect Harry Whittaker, specializes in the conservation of old buildings and he used his skills to create the beautiful shop and café from an old Dutch barn. Behind its kitchen is the mill where the flour is made, and customers can look through the glass and see the wheat being milled.

The shop is spacious and welcoming, with lots of natural light, fresh white walls, warm terracotta tiles and light wooden shelves. There is a wide range of produce for sale. Ginny tries to sell as much produce that is locally sourced as possible, although, in common with all organic shops, a large proportion of what she sells has to be imported, a trend she and other organic growers are seeking to change. Demand outstrips what we can produce in this country, and the public has also become used to produce being available out of season.

As well as fresh fruit and veg, including potatoes grown on the farm, the farm shop offers milk from their own herd. The selection of fresh cheeses is outstanding (the Staffordshire, made by the Deaville family, is a favourite, as is the wonderful blue Grinzola) and Pimhill's home-produced quiches, pies and frozen ready-meals are really popular. The frozen-food cabinets are full of meat and poultry of every sort, including game, wild boar and ostrich, as well as burgers and sausages. A large range of groceries is available, too, with tinned food, jams and pickles, cakes, biscuits and cereals, mostly organic and all GM free (see p 85). The shop boasts one of the best-stocked organic off-licences I have come across, with organic wines from as far afield as Australia and New Zealand. There are also attractive, environmentally friendly gifts such as stationery, cosmetics and candles; and a newly introduced herb garden, by Jane Bygott of Oak Cottage Herbs, can provide rare, historical herb varieties to customers, too.

Organic flour, made from wheat grown and milled at Pimhill.

A pine staircase behind the delicatessen counter leads up to the gallery café, where photographs of Pimhill, past and present, and shelves full of old books on farming and the countryside create a homely and friendly atmosphere. The café chefs change the menu regularly, and there are always unusual and original soups, savouries, quiches and sandwiches, as well as homemade bread and cakes. The flour used for all the cooking done here is Pimhill's own, milled on the premises from their own wheat.

To make life as easy as possible for Pimhill's customers, the shop and café are open seven days a week and there is ample car parking, a picnic area and good space and equipment for children to play. Ginny wants to sell far more home produce in the shop and also wants to introduce a new vegetable box sheme. To do this, two new barns have been built to create a collection, packing and distribution centre, and Michael Westrip, former head gardener at the Henry Doubleday Research Association's organic garden centre at Ryton-on-Dunsmore, near Coventry (see pp 57–64), has been appointed to oversee the growing of an extensive range of vegetables in the farm fields and in polytunnels. Once grown, the vegetables will be boxed up and sent out by van. This will be the first time that the farm has had a delivery service since the 1930s, when milk was delivered, and Ginny is delighted to be reviving an old tradition. Customers within a 20-mile radius will be able to place a regular order for boxes of specially selected, seasonal, organic vegetables and have them brought to their doors.

Pimhill's history goes back to the Domesday Book, when the first house was built on the site in 1196. Lea Hall, the rambling house with oak-panelled rooms and blazing fireplaces where Ginny, Harry and their three daughters Jessie, Nell and Chloe now live, was built in 1584 by Richard Lee. (One of his descendants was Robert E. Lee, the Confederate General during the American Civil War, so the Mayalls are occasionally visited by Americans tracing family origins!)

Ginny's grandfather, Sam Mayall, son of a mill-owner in Lancashire, contracted tuberculosis as a young man and doctors recommended an outdoor lifestyle. He bought Pimhill in 1923 and, with little knowledge of farming, began a new career. His first herd of Ayrshires, which arrived by cattle train from Scotland, became only the second tuberculin-tested herd in the area and in the 1930s the Mayalls sold milk direct from the farm. Ginny's father, Richard, joined Sam on the farm just after the war. While he had been studying agriculture in Glasgow, a fellow student had lent him a book about sustainable methods of farming. Both he and Sam became convinced that caring for the land and animals without the use of chemicals and pesticides was the correct way to farm, and in 1949 they abandoned their use altogether. They were viewed with considerable scepticism by their

Just some of the many temptations found in Pimhill's farm shop.

neighbours but, as an indication of how times have changed, a neighbour has recently converted to organic practices himself.

Although the family own the land, Richard Mayall sees himself very much as a steward for future generations. Conservation is vital to him, and he has an ongoing policy of tree and hedge planting and has also created ponds to encourage wildlife. He is committed to passing on the land in a better state than when he inherited it and was delighted that when Ginny took over the reins she shared his views. Richard felt that the business was hers to run as she saw fit, and happily Ginny's passion for the farm and organic practice was, and is, as strong as her father's and her grandfather's.

At Pimhill's farm shop, created from an old Dutch barn, Ginny tries to sell as much local produce as she can.

Pimhill is very much a family business and although Ginny is now in charge her parents still live close by and remain actively involved in the business. One of the great pleasures in running a farm organically is that it creates employment, and Ginny and others like her provide jobs for local people. 'I think one of the things I'm good at is delegating work to people who I know will do it much better than I can,' she says with characteristic modesty. She is always quick to appreciate and praise her staff.

After lunch on the day of my visit, we walked the new farm trail. In March, organic dairy farmers begin chain-harrowing, a process which uses chains to spread muck (put on the land in February) while the tines of the harrow scratch out weeds and generally aerate the grass. Once done, the grass is rolled to prepare it for cutting and grazing when the cattle go out in April.

All farmers love the day the cattle go out after the winter. It's a sight Pat and Tony Archer always enjoy, and Ginny can't wait to get hers out, as the protein count in the milk will improve when the cows start to eat the new spring grass. Richard says he notices that the cows themselves seem to look forward to the big day, too. They seem to be more alert and gaze longingly out at the fields. A firm believer in folklore, he says he watches for misty mornings in March, as the old saying 'As many mists in March come frosts in May' is invariably true. When Ginny worries that there is not enough vital clover in the spring grass, her father will stand anywhere in the field and if he can count four clover plants from any one spot, he knows there will be enough later in the season. He's never been wrong. I was interested

to see that chicory and plantain had been planted in the grass as well as the clover. These root more deeply than grass, which helps improve the soil, and they also contain extra minerals which are good for the cows and give them a variety of flavours to tuck in to.

The trail took us down the hill along the side of a field of wheat, where we admired the newly laid hawthorn hedge. Hedge-laying is part of Pimhill's ongoing conservation management. It is an exceptionally skilled job, involving weaving partly cut trunks and branches through the upright stems of the hedgerow. Ginny is lucky to have Alf Davies, a real expert in this old country craft, whose work can be seen all round the farm. Well-maintained hedges provide excellent habitats for wildlife, and there were badger setts underneath to prove this.

Some of the wheat Ginny grows is Maris Widgeon, an old-fashioned variety, much liked by organic farmers, as it grows exceptionally tall. This helps to keep out light, and so discourages weeds. Weeding is ever a problem for organic farmers, but some years ago Ginny invested in a mechanical weeding machine, and she showed us where it had recently been used. It takes great precision and skill to pass between the rows, and Fred, the son of a German prisoner of war who worked at Pimhill during the Second World War, does it admirably. From the trail you look across the fields and can see the different crops of cereal, oats, spring beans and potatoes. Information boards along the route, designed by the Soil Association (see p 100), explain the three-year crop rotation, which is an essential part of organic farming (and of course gardening), as it helps improve soil fertility and prevents the build-up of weeds and disease.

From the fields the trail leads into Rabbit Hill Wood, which was planted in 1966 and consists mainly of sycamore, ash and Scots pine. The Mayall family worked hard, with the Soil Association's guidance, clearing paths and installing fences and gates so that the different species of trees and any signs of wildlife are clearly evident. March is the last tree-planting month of the year and Richard's passion for it is apparent – there are lots of newly planted young oaks (protected by rabbit guards) to be seen. There are also nesting boxes to encourage the birds, fixed using wooden dowels rather than nails as these are less damaging to the trees.

The view from the gate at the edge of the wood is spectacular, and beyond the farm buildings the beautiful old Elizabethan farmhouse stands high and impressive. An Elizabethan barn has been lovingly restored and renovated under Harry's supervision as part of Pimhill's celebrations for 50 years of organic farming. It will be a splendid setting for parties and functions, but its main purpose will be to provide an education centre for the farm trail scheme.

The inspiration to take part in the scheme came when Jessie, Ginny's eldest daughter, went on a school visit to a farm. The children were constantly told not to touch things and many areas of the farm were firmly out of bounds. Ginny believes that children must be well supervised but still be able to have what she calls a really 'touchy-feely' experience on her farm trail. Guided by Ali Stevenson, Pimhill's Education Officer, they have the opportunity to collect items along the way so that they can learn from what they have seen, creating pictures and collages back at the barn. Young children learn far more from what they do than from what they are told, and Ginny wants them to have a really memorable and fun day at her farm.

Shotton Farm – the farm on the estate where the dairy cows are milked.

At Pimhill children can see the whole cycle of food production, from the wheat growing in the fields, to being milled and turned into flour, then made into bread and cakes in the kitchen, and finally they can taste it to experience for themselves how delicious it is. They can see the benefits of organic farming in terms of wildlife habitats and the environment, and there is hope that the message will reach a whole new generation. Judging from some of the letters Ginny has already received, this is happening.

Pimhill has been a great help and inspiration to *The Archers* storyline and the Mayalls' influence has led Pat to re-open a farm shop. So I ended my

Nell (left) and Jessie, Ginny's children, feeding their pet lambs. Old wine bottles are being recycled as animal feeding bottles!

visit... where else but in the shop! I couldn't resist buying a little of everything, and stocked up for the week. If I lived closer, I'd hardly ever go to a supermarket again. I had a marvellous day at Pimhill, and I look forward to returning to see how the farm develops and how new schemes progress. Ginny is already expanding her cattle herd through a partnership with a neighbouring farm and Pimhill is always changing and developing because they welcome feedback and ideas from friends and customers. She sends a regular newsletter about the farm to an ever-expanding mailing list, which I have joined. Interestingly, the motto of the Lee family, the original owners of Pimhill, was, 'Non incautus futuri', which means 'Always mindful of the future'. A motto which could have been created specially for Ginny Mayall.

practical organics

In the first month of spring, root veg and winter greens are still a good basis for cheap, wholesome suppers. Start emptying your freezer to make space for the new season's offerings. As the days lengthen and the weather warms up, it's time to start sowing seeds.

What to try in
march

Vegetables
Artichokes
Aubergines
Broccoli *(i)*
Cabbage
Cucumber
Herbs *(i)*
Kale
Leeks
Lettuces *(i)*
Mushrooms
New potatoes *(i)*
Purple sprouting
 broccoli *(i)*
Rocket
Root veg
Spinach
Tomatoes

Fruit
Bananas *(i)*
Citrus fruit *(i)*
Grapes *(i)*
Pears *(i)*
Rhubarb

FOR THE SHOPPER

March can be a lean month when it comes to buying vegetables. It's often too early for most British spring veg and winter produce is starting to run out. Many shops and organic vegetable box schemes will use imported supplies of fruit and veg in order to offer you some variety. Alternatively, try some of the organic frozen vegetables that are becoming more available.

Onions, carrots and potatoes can start sprouting around March as part of the spring growth spurt. Non-organic vegetables are spray-ed with chemicals to prevent this, but organic vegetables aren't. To avoid unwanted sprouts, store root vegetables in a cool dark place and use them up quickly. Naturally sprouting vegetables like purple sprouting broccoli begin to appear now, too, and citrus fruits are still in season from Europe to add some zest to your cooking.

Organic milk, with its distinct and delicious flavour is now widely available in shops.

Focus: Milk

With the spectre of BSE (bovine spongiform encephalopathy) all too vivid in many people's minds, many shoppers are turning to organic milk. Ginny Mayall describes it as the Rolls Royce of milks and anyone who has compared it with non-organic milk will agree. Organic milk is utterly delicious with a unique flavour and texture. It's widely available in supermarkets or direct from independent farmers and co-ops and is an excellent example of how you can support organic farming by what you choose to buy.

Taste the difference

The taste difference is a result of the importance placed on the health and well-being of organic dairy cows. When you buy organic milk, you can guarantee that it comes from cows who have been well looked after, as organic cows must be allowed to graze freely and are not allowed to be kept inside all the time. Farmers are encouraged to house them in open cowsheds, where they can wander about, rather than in cramped cubicles. Organic calves are weaned on to organic whole milk, preferably maternal, for a period of 3 months. A minimum of 51% of this must be natural organic milk, but they can use milk replacer provided this is also organic. Conventionally reared calves may be raised on milk or milk replacer which isn't organic and may contain additives or supplements such as antibiotics or marsarine.

Organic dairy herds graze on pastures free from synthetic pesticide sprays and fertilizers. Farmers pay close attention to building up the fertility of the soil naturally, by planting crops such as clover with the grass, and they use only natural fertilizers such as natural rock phosphate, calcified seaweed and ground limestone – naturally occurring minerals which put vital nutrients into the soil to help feed the plants growing there.

The cows eat a mainly organic diet, although up to 15% of non-organic feed is permitted. This will be gradually phased out by 2006. Feed content is strictly regulated, though, so you can be sure that organic milk cows have not consumed meat, fish or bonemeal, or anything genetically modified.

Organic farmers are opposed to the use of BST (bovine somatrophin), a growth hormone widely used in the USA to enhance milk yields. The avoidance of the overuse of antibiotics, something which is thought to be a factor in the worrying rise of antibiotic resistance in humans, is another important aspect of managing an organic dairy herd. In non-organic herds when cows are 'dried off', prior to giving birth to the next calf, they are given routine antibiotics to prevent infection. Ginny, and other organic dairy farmers, always uses homeopathic and herbal treatments, only resorting to antibiotics if there is no alternative.

Maintaining high standards of hygiene, minimizing stress and disturbance caused to animals, and many other common-sense measures are the real key to having healthy cows, says Ginny. 'It's to do with prevention rather than cure. The secret is to know your animals so you can recognize any problems early and nip them in the bud.'

The green top alternative?

Until the 1880s when railways could transport milk from farms to towns, people in urban areas got their milk from cows kept behind shops or on local green areas and/or commons, or from herds on the edge of town. Once transport was available, heat treatment of milk – pasteurization (named

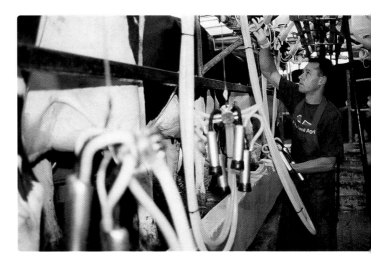

Dairy cows supplying organic milk are reared with great concern for their health and welfare.

TIP: BOXING CLEVER

A good way to get started if you are new to organic shopping is to join a box scheme. This means that each week you buy a box of assorted seasonal vegetables – either direct from the farmer/grower, from a distribution company, or increasingly from supermarkets – which is delivered to your door. Your box will always contain a selection of staple vegetables such as potatoes and onions and added to these will be whatever green vegetables are in season, some seasonal salad ingredients and perhaps one or more unusual vegetables. Veg box suppliers can nearly always deliver fruit boxes, too, or some may offer combined fruit and veg boxes (see p 68) as well as other organic goodies.

after Louis Pasteur, who showed it was possible to reduce bacteria by heating) – was introduced on a commercial scale in the 1920s. Today, virtually all milk sold in the UK undergoes some sort of heat treatment, including organic milk. Non-heat-treated milk is called 'green top' (not to be confused with the green caps and labels sometimes used to identify semi-skimmed milk). Green top milk can still be sold, provided it meets strict microbiological criteria, from the farm gate or through some registered milkmen, labelled 'This milk has not been heat treated and may therefore contain organisms harmful to health'.

Most organic milk is pasteurized to kill bacteria. However, some claim that green top milk is healthier, more flavoursome and nutritious than other milks, including organic. It's claimed that heat treatment used in pasteurization destroys valuable vitamins and minerals and also affects the body's ability to absorb folate, a vital vitamin needed for healthy blood and nerves and for embryo development during pregnancy. It's also thought it could trigger allergic reactions.

Most of the 400 or so dairy farmers in the UK who produced green top milk in 1999 are under pressure from the government to discontinue sales of the milk, although unpasteurized milk is still widely used for producing cheese. Ginny Mayall has, under great duress, temporarily stopped selling green top milk to the public, but she and her family still consume it themselves and she would love to sell it again. You may get it from some farmers' markets in England and Wales. For up-to-date information on availability, contact the Association for Unpasteurized Milk Producers and Consumers, Hardwick House, Hardwick Estate, Whitchurch, Reading RG8 7RB (tel: 0118 9842955).

Note: The government warns that babies, pregnant women and elderly or infirm people should avoid unpasteurized milk, cream and cheeses.

Know your milks

Milk labelling can be confusing as milk is categorized according to its fat content *and* by how it's been treated.

High or low fat?
Channel Islands milk: Has highest fat content of 5.2%.
Whole milk: Has a fat content of 3.9%, with nothing added or taken away. Recommended for children under five, who should not be given low-fat varieties of milk.
Standardized milk: The fat content has been standardized to be a minimum of 3.5% in accordance with EU regulations.
Semi-skimmed milk: Contains a fat content of between 1.5 and 1.8%. All the protein, calcium and most vitamins are retained but there is a reduction in the fat-soluble vitamins A and D.
Skimmed milk: Has a fat content of between 0.1 and 0.5%. Vitamins A and D are removed with the fat, so it is not suitable for babies and small children.

Putting on the heat
Homogenized milk: Treated to evenly distribute the fat globules throughout the milk.
Organic milk: Has generally been pasteurized and comes from cows reared organically.
Pasteurized milk: Treated by a process which involves heating it to a minimum of 71.7C to destroy a variety of micro-organisms including the one causing tuberculosis in cattle (once the source of TB in humans).
Sterilized milk: Is sealed in a container and heated for 10–30 minutes before being cooled. It is not completely sterile, in the strict sense of the word, and is less popular today than other heat-treated milks.
Unpasteurized (green top) milk: Has not been subject to treatment to destroy micro-organisms.
UHT milk: Ultra Heat Treated milk has been heated to over 138C to make it last longer. The process causes less chemical change than conventional sterilization yet the milk is almost completely sterile.

FOR THE GROWER

Now is the time to start sowing your vegetable seeds. Get some containers – flowerpots, clean old yogurt pots, modules or seed trays – with holes in the bottom and some sowing compost. Look for peat-free, organic compost as peat production destroys vast areas of the countryside. Organic compost such as mushroom compost, composted bark and various organic composite compost mixtures made with ingredients such as coir fibre and seaweed extract are available from garden centres or mail order through catalogues such as Chase Organic's (see p 190). HDRA produces leaflets on growing from seed and composting, and sells activators, that get your compost heap (see pp 69–70) off to a flying start.

Parsley sown now, and again in late summer, will give you a year-round supply.

Sowing organic seeds is just like sowing non-organic ones. Ideally seeds should be organic – try Terre de Semences (see p 190) – but if you can't get hold of them, conventional non-organic seeds come with or without chemical preservatives (to prevent deterioration), and a good alternative to organic seeds are non-treated ones which you can get from most good seed suppliers or from Chase's *Organic Gardening Catalogue* (see p 190).

Focus: Sowing seeds

Always follow any packet instructions or guidance that your gardening book gives you, but the basics of growing organic seeds are much like growing any non-organic ones. If you're a first-timer, modules (trays with separate 'cells') are a simple way to raise young plants for transplanting into the garden. They allow each young plant space to grow and, because its roots are not disturbed when you plant them out, they grow more quickly. Fill trays with compost and water from the top. Place a single seed or two in each module. Cover with clingfilm, a clear lid or a sheet of glass which should be moved and wiped daily, and leave on a sunny windowsill.

Once you spot the first green tips peeping above the surface of the compost remove the lid

---

TIP: FLEECE

A real ally, fleece is a lightweight, spun-polyester material and protects plants from pests and wind. The soil under it stays moist, so you still need to weed. Buy from garden centres or by mail order (see p 190).

Growing under polythene enables salad greens to be available earlier in the growing season than they would if grown out in the open.

Seeds to sow

Broad beans: A really nutritious vegetable. The Sutton is an ideal variety to grow in a small garden as it's only 30 cm tall. Aquadulce Claudia is the hardiest variety, or try Express if you want quick results.

Carrots: Sow in succession for a constant supply year-round. Try Nantes, sown now, for eating in June.

Celery: Best sown under glass at a temperature of 16C/60F. Golden Self-blanching is a dwarf variety which should be ready in August.

Leeks: Easy to grow and don't take up much room. Try King Richard, an early variety with a long stem, ideal for slicing for late summer use.

Lettuce: Sow at two-week intervals to give you a steady supply all summer long. There's a huge variety to choose from, so get busy with the seed catalogues and choose a few different varieties.

Onions: Onion seed can be sown direct into the ground or grown under glass. Try Ailsa Craig, a large, golden, straw-coloured onion.

Spring onions: Try White Lisbon and sow in succession from March right through the growing season.

Parsley: It's slow to germinate, but sow in spring and again in late summer for a year-round supply. Try flat-leaved French parsley or curly Campion Moss.

Peas: Sow wrinkled seed varieties in succession to produce peas until September. Ambassador is a good one to try, or Cavalier, a new maincrop variety with good resistance to powdery mildew. Banff is a vigorous early variety suitable for using fresh or freezing.

Potatoes: For maincrop try Arran Victory with their vivid blue/purple skins. They are wonderfully tasty and have some resistance to blight. Plant Nicola, a modern salad variety with an excellent yield, and Nadine, a second early potato which is waxy and cooks well.

Shallots: Sow now to harvest in August. Try Golden Gourmet, a yellow-skinned variety that keeps well, Longor (French with a red tinge and mild flavour) and Sante, an organic variety with a high yield that keeps well.

Tomatoes: Start them off indoors from late March onwards. Try Ailsa Craig, red and flavoursome, Aromata, an organic hybrid developed for north-west Europe, Gardener's Delight, a cherry tomato that crops well, the ever-reliable Moneymaker (now available as organic) and Marmander Super, a lovely bush tomato which, full of flavour, slices well and is good in salads.

or clingfilm from your containers and, if the compost is dry (probe gently with your finger to feel it), gently water seedlings from the base, taking care not to damage the fragile tips.

When your seedlings have grown about four leaves, stand them outside to get some light and air and to start getting them used to colder conditions. (This is 'hardening off' and can go on well into April, depending on the weather.) Choose a mild, sunny day to begin with and bring them in at night. If it's a mild evening, you can leave them out overnight but cover them with some sheets of newspaper or fleece to protect them against a potential frost. Once they have hardened off a bit – usually after about a week to 10 days, depending on the weather conditions during that time – and start showing threads of white root at the bottom of the module, push them from the module by pressing from below, and transplant them into the garden soil.

Garden jobs for March

- Sow seeds (see opposite)
- Plant maincrop potatoes, asparagus, Jerusalem artichokes, onion sets and garlic
- Plant perennial herbs such as marjoram, mint, rosemary and sage
- Sow green manures – *phacelia*, buckwheat, red clover, lupins, mustard, winter tares and trefoil
- Finish pruning and planting fruit bushes such as autumn-fruiting raspberries
- Graft apples and pears
- Continue greasebands until end of the month
- Cover ground under pear trees with carpet mulch to prevent pear midges
- If frosty, protect blossom with sacks or fleece
- Inspect raspberry canes for signs of raspberry moth and other pests and diseases

---

If you're a first-time organic gardener your soil won't have its full complement of soil micro-organisms, but by avoiding artificial chemicals and adding compost you'll build up its fertility.

Broccoli and potato gratin

Purple sprouting is richer in vitamin C than the average orange and is also high in calcium, folic acids, vitamins A, B_{12} and E.

Preparation time: 20 minutes
Cooking time: 1 hour 10 minutes
Serves: 4

450 g organic waxy potatoes, e.g. Cara
1 organic garlic clove, peeled and finely chopped
2 tbsp chopped fresh organic thyme leaves
1 tbsp organic olive oil
225 g organic purple sprouting broccoli
175 g organic blue cheese, crumbled
250 ml organic double cream
25 g organic breadcrumbs
Seasoning to taste

1. Pre-heat oven to 180C/350F/Gas 4. Cut the potatoes into wedges and put in a roasting tin. Sprinkle over the garlic, half the thyme, the oil and seasoning. Cook for 30–35 minutes until tender.
2. Meanwhile, cut off and slice lengthways the thicker broccoli stems. Blanch, with the broccoli heads, in lightly salted boiling water for 1 minute. Drain well and dry with kitchen paper. Arrange in a buttered 1.2-litre (2-pint) baking dish with the potato wedges and two-thirds of the blue cheese.
3. Mix half the remaining blue cheese with the cream and the rest of the thyme and season well. Pour over the vegetables. Sprinkle the breadcrumbs and remaining cheese over the top and bake for 30 minutes until golden and crusty.
4. Serve with crusty bread and baked tomatoes.

april

In 1985, on a bare, windswept site at Ryton-on-Dunsmore, a tv series on organic gardening, *All Muck and Magic?*, was filmed. Over four years, Alan and Jackie Gear showed viewers how to grow organic flowers, fruit and vegetables in an average urban garden.

It made tv personalities of the Gears and the staff of the Henry Doubleday Research Association (HDRA) for organic gardening. Their Ryton gardens demonstrated practical organic gardening on a small plot with only a pond, compost heap and patio area.

The Ryton site was certainly not chosen for its natural beauty, and the original 22 acres were flat and featureless. However, the ground had been used for horses and had not been farmed with chemicals and pesticides, and there was space and potential to create the biggest demonstration organic gardens in the UK. With much hard work and perseverance that is exactly what the Gears and their staff did.

Today Ryton has over 30 demonstration gardens on the site, immaculately cared for, beautifully designed, and flourishing, without a chemical in sight, and a visit there never disappoints. There is always something different and new to see, not only because of the changing seasons, but also because new gardens are always being developed and created alongside the old favourites like the *All Muck and Magic?* garden, which is still one of Ryton's most popular attractions.

Taking its name from a nineteenth-century Quaker smallholder, Henry Doubleday, who introduced a herb called Russian comfrey to Britain, and spent years experimenting with it as an instant organic compost base and soil improver,

57

The Cook's Garden, one of HDRA's newer gardens, growing herbs and salad plants in a beautifully designed space.

the Henry Doubleday Research Association was founded in 1958 by Lawrence Hills. The organization was made up of a small group of enthusiastic amateurs experimenting with organic techniques in their own gardens, but Hills needed people with scientific backgrounds to really make headway with his work.

Alan and Jackie Gear had met in 1968 as students at the University of Wales in Swansea. Like many students then, they became involved with CND and other protest groups and did their share of marching to try to change things and make a difference. After graduating, Jackie as a zoologist, and Alan as an engineer, they got jobs and bought a house and a car, but soon felt that they should be putting back more into the world and the environment. In 1974, organic gardening guru Hills placed an advertisement in *The Times* for 'a young couple to work on an organic trial ground – full board – no pay'. Jackie and Alan were just what he was looking for, and answering the advert they managed to haggle and negotiate a 'salary' of £5 a week each, and took the job. Hills feared their pay would bankrupt the organization, but history has proved that the Gears were probably the best investment he ever made.

Jackie and Alan's decision to sell their house and car and move to the tiny caravan on the site of the trial ground at Lawrence Hills's home at Bocking in Essex astonished their friends and families who thought they were eccentric cranks. Alan remembers winter life in the caravan as pretty uncomfortable and freezing cold. 'All the heat rose to the top, so you always had cold feet and an overheated head. The temptation was to go about on all fours, but it didn't seem practical!' However, they look back on those days with great affection.

Doing everything, from digging and cultivating to putting up buildings and coping with administration and correspondence, the Gears learnt about self-sufficiency, kept bees and chickens and grew vegetables and herbs. Under the guidance of Lawrence Hills's wife, Cherry, and with about 225 kg of fruit grown each year, Jackie became an expert in fruit bottling and preserving. She made jams and chutneys, developed skills in bread- and yogurt-making and learnt how to use herbs and make herbal remedies. The skills taught by Cherry Hills undoubtedly proved invaluable when Jackie later created a restaurant at Ryton.

Jackie was convinced that ordinary families needed to be able to see organic gardening in practice and learn techniques for themselves, and to do this the HDRA site needed to expand – what they were doing on the small site at Bocking needed to be done on a much larger scale in order to be able to spread the organic message more widely. A restaurant and shop were also an essential part of the plan, so that the public had a chance to sample good organic food, and the search began for a new site.

Wild marjoram blossoming in HDRA's Cook's Garden.

The move from Bocking to Ryton was a brave one, as they had no experience of cultivating gardens on such a large scale or of running a visitor centre with a shop and restaurant, but despite problems caused by the recession of the 1980s, the move to Ryton in 1985 succeeded. HDRA achieved what it had set out to do – creating their demonstration gardens and becoming a centre of vital information and resources for all organic growers – and today its membership stands at over 28,000. Its work and influence are internationally renowned, and when HRH The Prince of Wales began the organic conversion of his gardens at Highgrove, HDRA was called in to help and advise. The Prince became its Patron in 1989 and, following Ryton's success, a second demonstration garden centre was opened in 1995 at Yalding in Kent.

More organic horticultural research is done by HDRA than by any other organization in the UK. It is involved in numerous projects and works with many organizations to promote and develop organic practices.

HDRA works with the Ministry of Agriculture, Fisheries and Food (MAFF), developing sites in various parts of the UK to study pest control and the marketing of organic fruit and vegetables. They hope that they will one day be able to persuade the country's major vegetable producers in East Anglia to grow organically and lessen the need to import so much organic produce. HDRA aims to promote organic principles everywhere, be it in ornamental municipal gardens or school grounds. Their nearest city, Coventry, is aiming to manage all its green areas and gardens organically and HDRA want to see this trend grow and develop in other towns and cities, extending to grounds around everything from supermarkets to stately homes.

In 1999 HDRA began an exciting new project with English Heritage at Audley End, a stately home in Essex. The gardens here were landscaped by Capability Brown in the eighteenth century, and a walled kitchen garden was created in the nineteenth century. Sadly the gardens became neglected over time, and the property was eventually sold to the Historic Monuments Commission (now English Heritage) in order to pay death duties. The

Early maturing 'Matina' and 'Dwarf Double' tomatoes, companion planted with marigolds for organic pest control.

gardens were opened to the public at Easter 1999, although much restoration work was still to be carried out. The aim is to restore the kitchen garden to its former glory and to produce vegetables and fruit, as before, including heritage vegetables of varieties that have been lost over the years, and this time it will be done organically. The Victorians used to put all manner of undesirable substances on their gardens, including arsenic and nicotine, which would be deeply scorned today and HDRA are applying their skills and knowledge to help with the restoration work. A shop has been opened at Audley End selling plants and vegetables the gardens produce and, with the emphasis on history, care and effort is being put into producing goods aesthetically in keeping with the period. Glass (instead of plastic) cloches are being sourced and used in the gardens with cotton (instead of nylon) for garden netting.

HDRA's Heritage Seed Library is doing valuable work saving and preserving endangered flowers, fruits and vegetables.

Jackie wants HDRA to work more with garden centres and has put in a lottery bid to fund a Centre of British Vegetable Heritage, to complement the work they are doing to save and preserve forgotten varieties, both at Audley End and through the Heritage Seed Library at Ryton. The latter has done much to preserve seeds that have been threatened with disappearance because of European legislation, and because big seed companies cease production of all but really popular varieties. Heritage seeds cannot be sold, but are distributed to Library members through a Lost and Found service. Old varieties are being found again, and members receive information of these finds through newsletters. Many volunteer to become Seed Guardians to look after, and bulk up, supplies of seeds for storage at Ryton and distribution to members. A Seed Library catalogue is published annually and from it members may chose up to seven varieties to grow themselves.

As well as all this, HDRA has International Research and Overseas Development Departments to carry out important work all over the world, and have been involved in organic projects in India, Africa and Cuba. They have an Information and Education Department which answers thousands of enquiries by phone, letter and e-mail every year, and sends out tens of thousands of fact sheets, which are constantly being updated. Staff regularly appear on radio and tv spreading the word, and write regularly in national newspapers and magazines.

The restaurant at Ryton. The opportunity for a relaxing and delicious break during a tour of the gardens.

At Ryton itself, the award-winning shop and restaurant go from strength to strength. The menu changes regularly, with original recipes created from fresh ingredients, both vegetarian and non-vegetarian. The shop and restaurant were both very much Jackie's babies, and she trained local staff so successfully that the restaurant acquired an entry in the *Good Food Guide*. There is currently a big demand for organic catering, and so in order to run the enterprise even more efficiently, on a larger scale, the management has been handed over to a specialist chef.

Each time I go to Ryton I am reminded of the amazing energy and dedication of the Gears and all their staff. Their enthusiasm would encourage even the laziest and most unwilling of gardeners to pick up a spade, and it is to their credit that HDRA now has the largest membership of any organic association in Europe. At each visit to Ryton I see the changes that have taken place since my last visit. This time I was particularly interested to look at two of the newer gardens, the Cook's Garden and the Paradise Garden.

I had seen the Cook's Garden (opened in 1998) during its construction and had talked to Kathleen Askew, the brilliant young gardener who both designed and built it. Her passion for gardening began when she worked at her local garden centre while still at school, and although she trained as a landscape gardener her real joy is not just the designing, but the creating of gardens. She has done a superb job with the Cook's Garden and it is a great tribute to her talent. The space is enclosed with low, curving brick walls incorporating arches and wooden benches, and there is a wonderful water feature whose lapping sound adds to the beauty of the garden. Kathleen has used warm terracotta tiles and bricks to create curving paths, and in the centre has built a stunning mosaic. The beds of rarer salad, fruit and herb plants fan out towards the edges of the small walled space and many of the tender young plants are protected by recycled plastic-bottle cloches, which do an excellent job. The whole is truly a delight to the eye, and the plants also add floral garnishes to the restaurant's stylish cookery.

I had also seen Geoff Hamilton's Paradise Garden once before, in the very early planning stage when rare breed sheep were doing their bit in its preparation by grazing and manuring the paddock, before digging work began. Geoff Hamilton, the much-loved and missed gardener of BBC tv's *Gardeners' World* fame, had been a friend and staunch supporter of HDRA for over 10 years before he died, and gave them frequent publicity in his tv programmes and magazine articles. Jackie and Alan were determined to create a garden in his name as a lasting tribute.

The Paradise Garden was designed by Isabella van Groeningen and Gabriella Pape of Land Art, and when I visited was in the final stages of construction by Bernhard's Landscapes and HDRA's staff. It is a glorious conception, combining a formal garden with neat paths, a greenhouse, pavilion and pergola, which merges with an informal country garden with wildflower meadow, trees and shrubs. The two are linked beautifully with water, in a landscaped pond and bog area. The Paradise Garden is aptly named, and all the materials used in its creation are environmentally friendly. The wooden pergola is made of green oak, which looks good and will last for years without the need for chemical preservatives. It will be entered by a fine old wrought iron gate which has been given by Geoff Hamilton's widow, Lynda, and used to hang at his home in Barnsdale. After my visit to Ryton for the research for this book I was fortunate, a few weeks later, to be at the opening ceremony of the garden. It was a joyful celebration

Paradise Garden, showing part of the wooden pergola made from green oak.

of Geoff's life and work attended by his family, friends and tv and radio celebrities, as well as HDRA members in their hundreds. It was a wonderfully happy occasion, which not even the British summer downpour could spoil.

HDRA has much to offer all gardeners, whether town or country based, with a small or large garden or allotment. Alongside expert advice on growing all kinds of flowers, vegetables and fruit, with special attention being given to different types of composting and natural methods of pest control, they offer a wealth of information about so many things. Their wildlife garden and conservation areas demonstrate the importance of encouraging birds and animals to deal with pests. They have gardens designed to promote gardening for people with visual and mobility disabilities, using highly scented flowers, easy wheelchair access and raised beds. And there is even a picnic area close to the Ornamental Kitchen Garden which gives visitors time to pause and reflect during their tour.

People come regularly to collect boxes or bags of locally grown produce, packed on site at HDRA, Ryton.

Special events, workshops and courses are regularly held on all types of gardening and cookery as well as on subjects like homeopathy and watercolour painting. One event, Potato Day, in February has become so successful that it is now one of their most important annual events. Over 100 different seed potato varieties are available, and tens of thousands of tubers are sold to members, who turn up from all over the country. Competition for the more unusual varieties is fierce, and tempers can get quite heated as supplies run short. So popular is the event, it now extends into two days every year. Summer fêtes and gardening weekends also attract large numbers.

I ended my visit in the shop. It sells a wonderful selection of fresh and frozen food and has introduced a box vegetable scheme which has attracted a quickly growing membership. It also has a comprehensive selection of garden tools and seeds, and one of the best bookshops for organic gardeners and cooks. It richly deserves the awards it has won.

Jackie and Alan lead their team at HDRA from strength to strength and have so many successful ventures to be proud of. Alan says he's sorry that, because he is so busy in the office, he rarely holds a spade now except for a photo shoot. He also admits to a pang of regret… public opinion towards organics has changed so much that nobody calls them cranks any more, and he says he has a lot of time for cranks. In an article in *HDRA News* he was quoted as saying, 'We passionately believe that organic growing offers the only truly sustainable way forward for mankind – our task is to make sure that the message gets through.' It's hard to imagine many who are working harder to achieve this than the Gears and their staff.

practical organics

With a bit of luck the worst of the winter weather should be over by April and the first spring vegetables will be making an appearance. Make the most of these, and seasonal fruit such as rhubarb, in your cooking. It's another busy month for sowing in the garden.

What to try in
april

Vegetables
Asparagus
Aubergines
Broccoli
Cauliflower
Cabbages
Carrots *(i)*
Celery
Courgettes
Cucumber
Mushrooms
Onions *(i)*
Spinach
Tomatoes

Fruit
Apples *(i)*
Bananas *(i)*
Citrus fruit *(i)*
Mangoes *(i)*
Pears *(i)*
Rhubarb

FOR THE SHOPPER

Root crops like potatoes and carrots are beginning to be in short supply this month. Sadly, the British weather means you'll probably have to wait another month or so before home-grown new crop potatoes, spring vegetables and salad leaves start to appear in any quantity. If you're lucky, though, and the weather's mild, you may find a few bunches of young spinach, spring onions and, towards the end of the month, baby carrots and asparagus on offer.

Some organic farmers use polytunnels – polythene structures that act like a greenhouse – in order to encourage crops that need warmer conditions than the average British field to grow a bit faster. So you may find tender vegetables such as aubergines, Chinese greens, courgettes and tomatoes grown in these tunnels becoming available now, or you may have to buy a few imported vegetables during April. Broccoli begins to appear now, too – it goes exceptionally well with cheese, especially blue cheese. Citrus fruits

The local advantage

Buying locally grown food, which is fresher, is also cheaper and a good way of helping care for the environment as it cuts down on fuel and packing costs. According to the Soil Association it's estimated that transportation and packaging of food accounts for 12% of the UK's total fuel consumption, so by buying your food locally you are helping to save the earth's precious resources and helping local employment, too.

are in season in Europe and they are wonderful for adding extra zest to many dishes.

Focus: Vegetables and salads

There is nothing quite as tasty and nutritious as an organic carrot or lettuce freshly dug from the earth and simply served. Non-organic vegetables have a uniformity of appearance and flavour, whereas the organic variety are individual in both. Don't expect perfection in organic vegetables: part of their charm is their sometimes odd shapes and sizes. Be prepared to find the odd creepy-crawly or snail too – this is simply a sign that all wildlife hasn't been zapped out of existence with pesticides. Make sure you inspect and wash organic produce thoroughly so that you don't find any surprises on your dinner plate! Because organic growers avoid using artificial fertilizers or pesticides and rely instead on building up the fertility of the soil, organic vegetables have to 'work harder' to grow. This means they tend to be less watery and more flavoursome, especially when freshly picked.

Trefoil, suppressing weeds under a sweetcorn crop.

The nutritional factor

It is hard to say definitively that organic vegetables have the edge on non-organic varieties nutritionally. Much depends on the quality of the soil they are grown in and the species of vegetable. What you can be certain of is that organic vegetables haven't been exposed to the artificial pesticides and fertilizers that are used in non-organic food production. Many of these are toxic and, despite controls on acceptable levels of pesticides and herbicides, research in 1997 showed that pesticide residues in food could be many times the recommended safety levels. What is more we still don't know the long-term effects of many of the chemicals used, how long they remain in the body or the effects of ingesting a cocktail of different chemicals. The advent of genetically modified crops is another worrying aspect, too (see p 85).

Another bonus of organic produce is that it tends to be fresher – especially if you grow your own or buy from the farm gate or a box scheme (see p 68). Nutrients like vitamin C are lost rapidly once a vegetable has been picked, so fresher produce can only be a good thing.

Where to buy?

There are various places you can buy your organic vegetables. The one you choose will depend on your budget, your tastes and your lifestyle. If you live in a city, for example, have a car, do most of your shopping in the supermarket, want a wide choice of vegetables and don't have to watch your budget too closely, then you may find it more convenient to buy your organic vegetables at the supermarket. If, on the other hand, you are on a tight budget, you may find it cheaper to go for a box scheme, visit a farmers' market or buy direct from the farm gate. If you're a connoisseur of

good food, you might also like a box scheme, as the veg are probably the freshest you will find anywhere. Often you are sent one or two odd items that you might never have thought to buy in a shop and you can taste something new and exciting. Some producer-run box schemes close altogether for a few months of the year when produce is not available and others rely on imports to keep supplies of fruit and veg flowing.

Supermarkets

The amount of organic produce in supermarkets has increased dramatically recently as a result of fears about the safety of our food. In 1997–99 the amount we spent on organic food doubled to £363 million. The major supermarkets now all sell a wide range of organic vegetables and fruit and the choice is increasing all the time. However, most import substantial amounts of produce and, at present, supermarkets tend to be more expensive because transport and storage costs are passed on to the consumer. Many supermarkets are actively encouraging their suppliers to go organic and prices are likely to become more competitive as more farmers make the transition.

Nearly organic

Farmers' markets have opened the opportunity for smallholders to sell direct to the public again. If you shop at one you may sometimes find stallholders selling organically grown food that is not certified. This is because official certification can be a costly and lengthy process for the small-scale producer and many are simply not in a postition, financially or commercially, to apply for an official licence. If in doubt, ask questions about their farming methods, or ask to visit so you can see for yourself.

Box schemes

Box schemes, supplying seasonal fruit and veg delivered to your door, are an excellent way of supporting local growers and can be an economical way of buying organic vegetables. The growers must be certified by the Soil Association or other organic body (see p 6) so if you are subscribing to a scheme, check that the farmer is certified.

There are basically two types of box schemes, producer-run ones and ones run by a company. Producer box schemes are run by organic farmers as a way of marketing their own produce direct to the consumer. Prices often compare to non-organic equivalents in supermarkets and vegetables are usually extremely fresh as many farmers pick in the morning and deliver in the afternoon. As a result you may really notice the difference in taste. The contents of the box will depend on the scheme you belong to. With some schemes you will have to take pot luck. However, many offer a degree of choice and let you list foods you dislike and a few favourites, so if you're a strawberry fan and there's a glut you may get a few extra punnets. To ensure you get a good selection it's worth asking the farmer how many vegetables he or she grows. Only about 70 vegetables grow in the UK, and any farmer who grows less than about 40 probably won't be able to offer you a great deal of choice. Apart from a few exotic vegetables grown in polytunnels the choice will be mainly traditional British, seasonal vegetables.

Company box schemes are run by wholesalers who buy in produce from various suppliers and also import vegetables. You are more likely to find them operating in towns and cities. They tend to be slightly more expensive than producer box schemes because the veg is not going direct from farmer to consumer, and produce may be slightly less fresh. The advantage is that you may

Bottle cloches, like these used at Ryton, recycle plastic and protect your tender young seedlings.

have more choice of exotic imported veg and some company schemes can also deliver products like organic flour and wine. Some supermarkets, such as Waitrose, are starting up box schemes too.

Farmers' markets

Over the past year there's been an explosion of farmers' markets throughout the UK so there's probably one near you. They are good sources of fresh, cheap, local food and although not all the produce sold is organic you'll generally find quite a few organic producers selling their wares. If you buy from a farmers' market that belongs to the National Association of Farmers' Markets, you can guarantee that products are locally grown or produced using at least one local raw ingredient. Only the producer, his or her family or someone directly involved in the growing/production of the food is allowed to sell it and only good quality and wholesome food should be sold. Packaging should be minimal or recycled.

FOR THE GROWER

This month you'll probably be sowing seeds for more vegetables and herbs and 'planting out' (transplanting into their permanent positions) cabbage, early potatoes, shallots, lettuce, cauliflower and onions that you started off indoors. For seeds to germinate outdoors the soil must be warm enough, so if weeds are beginning to flourish then you can be fairly certain that the soil is warm enough for your vegetables too. You can sow earlier provided you warm up the soil first by covering it with a cloche or black polythene for a week or so. If you haven't already got a compost heap, get one started, then you won't have to buy in organic compost to boost your soil fertility.

Focus: Soil fertility and compost

The whole essence of organic gardening is to build up the fertility of the soil so that artificial fertilizers are not needed. A healthy organic garden is largely achieved through the use of compost and manures.

Compost helps to lighten heavy soil, helps light soils retain more moisture, feeds plants and

> ### TIP: HARDENING OFF
>
> Your seedlings should be planted out as soon as their roots have filled their container, but first you need to get them used to the colder conditions outdoors. The best way to do this is to stand them out on a sunny day for a while. Each day let them stay out for longer and gradually, after about a week, they should be acclimatized and ready to plant outside.

helps control disease. It's very simple to make your own compost by recycling garden waste and scraps from the kitchen. Homemade compost is a great way to save money on soil improvers, fertilizers and mulches and it's also better for the environment as it cuts down on the amount of waste you throw into your dustbin. You can also use compost as one of the ingredients in making up your own homemade growing media for seeds and plants. In an ideal world, you would only use organic waste to make compost, however, anything that decomposes can be composted.

Do it yourself garden compost

If it rots, it composts. This is a simple rule of thumb when deciding what to put in your compost heap or bin. The best compost contains a mixture of different ingredients. Some, like grass from the lawnmower, rot down quickly and can be used as an activator to get your compost started. Older, tougher materials like tea bags, green hedge clippings and soft prunings take longer to rot down but are useful to give the compost body. Woody prunings, stalky hedge clippings and autumn leaves tend to rot very slowly, so it's a good idea to shred or chop them up first with shears, a spade or a shredder.

Manure matters

The word 'manure' makes most of us think of animal waste, but here we are talking 'green manures' that organic gardeners and farmers use. These are plants grown to enhance the richness and fertility of the soil and improve its structure. They have been used for centuries since before farming was industrialized, although until fairly recently they haven't been so widely used in gardens and allotments.

Green manures help break up heavy soils to allow more air in and improve drainage and they help light, sandy soils to retain water. They also nourish the soil. A heavy downpour can wash nutrients out of the soil and deplete its potential. Green manure crops absorb soil nutrients via their roots and store them, and their presence helps prevent the soil itself being washed away. Their leaves help break the force of the rain and keep temperature and moisture more evenly regulated – which is good for worms. Another bonus is that green manures look attractive and help smother weeds.

The idea is quite simple. Sow the green manure seeds – good ones to plant in April are alfalfa, buckwheat, clover, fenugreek, lupins, *phacelia* (a bushy plant with bright blue flowers) and mustard – and let the plants grow until you need the land for your carrots, cabbages or whatever. At this point you dig the manure crop into the soil, where it decomposes to release its nutrients to nourish your vegetables and other plants.

Making your compost heap

To make compost you can simply create a heap on the ground and cover it with plastic or a piece of old carpet to keep it moist, but most people use a compost bin. It's quite simple and cheap to make one – an old dustbin with the bottom cut out and turned upside down does the trick or simply drive four wooden posts into the ground, staple wire mesh to them, line with cardboard cartons and pop a square of carpet or plastic on top. You might prefer to buy a ready-made bin. Ideally it needs to be large enough to hold a decent amount of compost, rainproof (look for one with a sturdy lid) and should keep moisture and heat in. Bought bins hold about 300 litres but if you make your own you can make it larger.

Cold compost

Put your bin directly on the ground to allow water to seep out and let worms in. Ensure it's in a convenient spot where you'll be able to get to it easily. Add ingredients as and when they become available and leave them for a year or so to rot down.

It's best to add as much as you can at one time rather than adding single items frequently. Before adding to the bin, either mix all the ingredients together or layer different materials in 20–25-cm seams (like a sundae). Water the heap/bin if it is dry, as without moisture the

Compost trials on rye grass at HDRA, Ryton, where much research about organic issues is carried out.

material won't rot down. Keep it covered and leave it until the compost is soft and crumbly.

Hot compost

A quicker way to create compost (in about six months) is to make a 'hot' compost heap. This involves filling the bin in one go, then removing the contents every few weeks to turn and aerate them and speed up the decomposition process.

Collect material to fill the whole of your compost bin using manure, scraps from the market, weeds and so on, and using a mix of soft and tough items. (Tough items should be chopped up with shears or a shredder.) Mix the ingredients together well and add them to your bin, watering as you go about every 30–60 cm. Cover with carpet and a lid. Within a few days the heap will be hot to the touch – the micro-organisms breaking down the waste matter.

As it cools over the next week or so, turn the contents by removing everything and mixing it up. If it's dry, add water or if it's soggy, add more dry matter. Return everything to the bin and wait a week. If the heap gets hot again, repeat the mixing step until the heap no longer heats up. Leave the heap for composting to continue for a further few weeks until you have lovely crumbly compost.

Garden jobs for April

- Sow broad beans, French beans, runner beans, beetroot, leaf beet, peas, broccoli, sea kale, leeks, cabbage, turnips, spinach, spring onions, lettuce and other salad greens. If you're lucky enough to have a greenhouse, sow sweetcorn, marrows, squashes and cucumbers
- Hoe and weed as needed
- Sow green manures (see opposite)

Minted crème fraîche spring vegetables

There's something quintessentially spring-like about this recipe, which makes use of fresh young vegetables and herbs now in season. The delicate greens of the leeks, peas and lettuce go very well with a lightly dressed, bright, juicy tomato salad.

Preparation time: 10 minutes
Cooking time: 25 minutes
Serves: 4

25 g organic butter
1 tbsp organic olive oil
225 g organic baby onions
200 ml organic dry white wine
2 medium organic leeks, halved and cut into 5-cm ribbons
350 g organic frozen petits pois
3 heads organic baby gem lettuce, quartered lengthways
200 ml organic crème fraîche
2 tbsp chopped organic mint
2 tbsp chopped organic flat-leaf parsley
Seasoning to taste

1. Heat the butter and olive oil in a large non-stick frying pan until lightly foaming. Add the baby onions and cook over a low heat for 8 minutes. Add the wine and leeks and bring to the boil. Simmer for 5 minutes until the leeks are tender.
2. Add the petits pois, simmer for 5 minutes.
3. Add the lettuce and simmer for a further 3 minutes.
4. Stir in the crème fraîche and herbs. Season well. Warm through very gently for 2–3 minutes.
5. Serve spooned over hot, soaked bulghur wheat or steamed couscous.

may

Lizzie Vann is one of the pioneers in the organic babyfood market. Parents are demanding healthy, pure foods for their babies and in 1999 over 20% of the babyfoods sold in the UK were organic, with one in three babies now eating some organic babyfood in their first year.

Mothers today have the option of feeding their babies organic babyfood. None was available when my own children were babies, 20-odd years ago. Back then, jars and packets of processed babyfoods tasted bland and boring, baby rusks and biscuits were sweet, and labelling of ingredients seemed vague and uninformative. In order to avoid the additives, salt and sugar I was certain a lot of babyfoods contained, I had to purée and sieve fresh fruit and vegetables. This was a messy, time-consuming process, and I was a busy working mother. Babyfood recipe books were hard to come by, and although health visitors and baby clinics were helpful, I sometimes found it quite hard to give my babies a good variety of tasty nutritional food.

Things are very different now, and we have Lizzie Vann largely to thank for this. She founded Baby Organix babyfoods in 1992 and it now boasts 57 varieties, available nationwide in major chemists and supermarkets, as well as independent pharmacies and health food shops. Modern mums don't know how lucky they are! Between 1998 and 1999 sales of organic babyfood doubled, and Lizzie Vann's Baby Organix is pledged to making it ever more widely available.

I originally met Lizzie Vann in 1994 at the rather odd venue of Waterloo Station, at an Organic Harvest Breakfast, when Baby Organix was a fairly young company. Aware of the phenomenal growth and success of the organic babyfood market, I wanted to meet her again and write her story for this book. Before I did, though, during a telephone conversation I experienced the measure of her energy and commitment to her product when I mentioned that two members of *The Archers* cast had recently become mothers. She immediately sent them starter packs of babyfoods, which I duly delivered to the two delighted new mothers and their little boys. I was pleased to report to Lizzie when we did meet that she had two new fans.

Lizzie's home is Hillside Farm, near Christchurch in Dorset. She and her partner, Mike, bought the property at auction, and when I visited it was hard to believe that the attractive yellow and white, single-storey, wooden

The wonderful converted chicken house, home to Lizzie Vann, where she still creates some of her recipes on the kitchen Aga.

house, with its veranda full of tropical plants, had only three years before been a chicken shed. It has been beautifully converted, creating a lovely home full of bright primary colours, and it stands on a hill at the end of a very long drive with wonderful views of their farmland. Their 100 acres are farmed organically by a tenant farmer and Lizzie loves living on a farm. 'Every day when you come home something's changed,' she enthused to me.

Lizzie's bright open-plan kitchen, complete with Aga, is where most of her recipe development is done. I had assumed that the idea for setting up Baby Organix had been borne out of recipes and food ideas tried out on her own babies. I was wrong, but she admits that she did try out recipes on her three step-daughters during Sunday lunches round the kitchen table. The girls were in their teens at the time and, although patient and willing to help out, soon tired of 'mush' and demanded roast chicken again instead. Lizzie had invited me for lunch and as we talked was mashing vegetables. Perhaps I looked slightly perturbed as she said, 'Don't worry, this isn't all I'm giving you for lunch!' In fact she had a lovely leg of organic lamb from her friend and tenant farmer Ron Lakey's farm shop.

As a teenager, Lizzie had been in sympathy with organizations like Friends of the Earth and Greenpeace. She took a degree in Biology at Lancaster University and eventually went to work in the City as a merchant banker. She said it was an experience she wouldn't have missed, as she found learning about international money movements absolutely fascinating. She worked for some time in London before Chase Manhattan moved her to Bournemouth to the 'back office' – a move that was only intended to be for three months, but during this time Lizzie realized how much she hated living in London. She'd also met and fallen in love with Mike, who was running a graphic design consultancy, and so she decided to leave city finance and settle in Bournemouth.

Lizzie and Mike began to work together in food product development. They'd always been interested in food and health issues, and Lizzie had cured her own asthma and eczema using natural remedies. She bombarded large manufacturers with lots of ideas for healthy foods, suggesting fresh soups, low-fat biscuits and salads, all using the best possible ingredients. It quickly became clear to Lizzie and Mike that established food-processing factories couldn't cope with making the products

Lizzie Vann busy in her kitchen at home.

they had in mind. Not only were the factories keen to keep costs down by using cheaper ingredients, but they were also unwilling to invest in the technology needed. If a factory was designed to make tinned soup, then that was what it made. Lizzie pointed out to me an interesting conundrum… that 'big companies don't take big risks, it's the small companies who do that all the time'.

It emerged that supermarkets were keen to buy organic produce. Still without a manufacturer, Lizzie decided to produce a range herself and she and a colleague, Jane Dick, came up with the Organix brand name. They discovered that what the public wanted was a range of high-quality organic babyfood. Lizzie found that what was available at the time were bland and uninteresting ranges, with too many unnecessary additives. She believes passionately that babies deserve the best possible start in life, with the healthiest natural food available, and she is certain that organic food is vital in giving them this start. Recent research has shown that long-term health problems can result from the consumption of pesticide residues by young children, whose digestive systems are particularly vulnerable to such toxins.

In 1992 Baby Organix was set up to provide busy mothers with the highest quality babyfood, made from fresh, organic ingredients and supplied in convenient form. They're sold in 100 g jars for babies in the first stage of weaning, with larger jars for babies from seven months old and they also developed a Junior Range in 250 g jars for babies over 12 months. Lizzie and her team always quality-control the recipes, tasting them before passing them over to a nutritional expert for checking. Organix produces babyfood that is simple and nutritious, and tastes good.

The flavours and varieties available are interesting and original. Among first-stage favourites are Prune and Oatmeal, Tomato and Chicken Casserole and Banana and Blueberry, while the more sophisticated Vegetable and Coconut Korma, Banana and Mango Couli and Fruity Rice with Chicken and Apricots are very popular with older babies. Delicious fruit varieties and puddings (all without added sugar) are designed for all ages, and breakfast foods such as Banana Porridge come either in jars, or packets for mixing with milk. Pasta varieties sell really well, with Pasta Hoops, Pasta ABCs and even Pasta Stars! And there are baby breadsticks for teething toddlers that won't damage new teeth and gums as they contain no added sugar.

The babyfood jars are produced in the Baby Organix factory in Ely in Cambridgeshire, although the headquarters are still based in Christchurch. With their success they have expanded and recently moved into a bigger office. Lizzie now has a team of 20 working there, and regular visits are made to the factory to check on quality control. The team are diligent in their sourcing of high-quality ingredients and Lizzie says vegetables, in particular, are always subject to seasonal variations. She has also found problems sourcing organic chicken in large quantities. Mass producing chickens is difficult; and, as she says, it would be ideal if 'we all kept half a dozen or so in our own back yards, then they could be kept in better conditions'. At the moment, Organix do all their own sourcing, but Lizzie looks forward to the day when they might be able to employ a 'forager' who could travel worldwide to find out what's available.

Lizzie and her team liaise closely with mother and baby groups, work with health visitors and visit baby clinics to give talks and demonstrations. She listens to feedback and insists that their labelling must be accurate and informative. Organix was the first company in the UK to give ingredient percentages on its labels, so that mothers know exactly how pure the food is and what ratio of ingredients it contains. In order not to waste resources and materials, the bright, attractive packaging, designed by Mike, also includes useful information both inside and out on some of the packets.

Baby Organix won the Soil Association Best Organic Babyfood award each year from 1993 to 1999, in addition to winning Mother and Baby Awards for four years, and in 1997 the Caroline Walker Award for Promoting Better Health through Diet. They have also been winners of the ADAS (Agricultural Development and Advisory Service) marketing award for product excellence. Organix are dedicated to the health of babies, and have a Freephone Helpline (see p 189) where mothers can get expert help and information on any dietary problems or food allergies. They also produce excellent leaflets of their favourite recipes, so that mothers can create their own meals. Ideas for new products can come from

A view from Lizzie's house of the surrounding farmland.

anywhere, with the idea for the pasta ranges coming, in part, from an Italian mother who said she believed giving pasta to children helped with their speech development, as chewing forces the tongue backwards and forwards.

For lunch at Lizzie's we were joined by Ron and Lizzie Lakey, their farming neighbours who had provided the leg of lamb we were enjoying. Ron told me that, for many years, he had been concerned about the quality of the food we produce and had been farming his land using traditional methods (without agrichemicals) for several years before he applied for his official Soil Association registration. His 100-acre farm became fully certified as organic within one year of his application, thanks to the fact that he had never used fertilizers or sprays and, as Ron joked, 'With Lizzie (Vann) as a friend nagging me about it, I'd have been in trouble anyway!'

Ron also farms Lizzie and Mike's 100 acres at Hillside Farm in addition to his land at nearby Owl's Barn Farm. He has a small herd of cattle and 200 or so ewes, and has found that traditional Hereford cattle and Dorset Horn and Poll Dorset sheep suit his organic system best. He keeps a flock of Llanwenog sheep so that with the Dorset sheep lambing in the autumn and the Llanwenogs in the spring, he can produce lamb all year round. Selling most of his meat direct to the public through his farm shop has tripled Ron's income. The shop stocks fresh and frozen organic meat, as well as their own-recipe burgers and sausages and many other organic foods. As a licensed game dealer, Ron sells venison and other game. Going organic and opening the farm shop have been the keys to his recent success, and Ron has hardly felt the recent crisis in farming, caused by the huge drop in prices, that has affected most conventional farmers. He has expanded his shop owing to the huge increase in demand for his meat. Lizzie Vann has plans of her own for developing new enterprises and she has already planted a young orchard of which she is very proud.

Baby Organix's new spacious open-plan offices in Christchurch are situated on an island in the river, in premises rented from the Water Board. They have big meeting and conference rooms with space to display samples of their products and information leaflets. There is a large kitchen with a big freezer, and Lizzie plans to do some of the recipe testing here (in addition to that which takes place on her Aga at home). She and her staff

taste all new recipes, and the following day was going to be one of their tasting days, which they all enjoy.

Lizzie has a great team, and great products which the customers love, and they are all very proud of what they do. She is a firm believer in training courses for her employees, and trains them for new intellectual challenges and responsibilities. Her team are busy organizing distribution of products to supermarkets, visiting the factories and checking nutritional values of the products, as well as negotiating with suppliers of jars and packaging, not to mention keeping up with all the latest Freephone and Internet technology in order to ensure that customers have the best possible service.

Baby Organix is a major success story, largely thanks to the energy and commitment of Lizzie Vann and her team. The company now has a turnover of some £5 million. Thanks to this success, Organix has been in a position to sponsor the Soil Association's Organic Food and Farming Report for the past two years, which Lizzie is proud and happy to do. She is still committed to the original ideals of the company and passionate that children should be given a healthy diet from the very start. She admits that the success of Baby

Cattle owned by Ron Lakey, Lizzie's neighbour, who farms Lizzie and Mike's farmland organically.

Organix certainly tests management ability, and that handling the growth of the company can sometimes make them feel vulnerable. 'True character comes out with success,' she says and she feels that she could, one day, sell out her shares to one of the major babyfood companies. But for now she doesn't want to go down that path as she still wants to be able to provide customers with something unique. They can't compete with the big companies in terms of prices on the shelves, but what they offer mothers and babies is the *best* – the best recipes, made with the best ingredients and guaranteed GM free.

Lizzie was recently awarded a much-deserved MBE for services to organic food. She is looking to the future, and is exploring various possibilities like exporting, or developing other outlets – maybe mother and baby cafés attached to children's clothing chains. She has also launched a range of organic frozen food for older children, including sausages and beefburgers. She told me that she would love to work with schools and also has ideas for a visitor centre on the farm one day, if she can get planning permission. Based on the stunning success of Baby Organix since its creation in 1992, I'm sure that when she's ready and wants to, Lizzie Vann will come up with another winner. In the meantime mothers throughout the land should offer up a big vote thanks for the wonderful and original range of babyfoods she has created.

New lambs – Ron Lakey's Poll Dorsets.

practical organics

With its long and, hopefully, sunny days May is a fantastic month for the cook and the gardener. It's a month to enjoy being outside and coming home to simple meals based around the first of the delicate, tender summer vegetables.

What to try in
may

Vegetables
Asparagus
Beetroot
Broad beans
Carrots
Courgettes
Fennel
Globe artichokes
Kohlrabi
Leeks
Lettuce
New potatoes
Radishes
Spinach
Spring cabbage
Spring onions

Fruit
Avocados *(i)*
Gooseberries
Grapes *(i)*
Mandarins *(i)*
Melons *(i)*
Rhubarb
Satsumas *(i)*
Strawberries *(i)*

FOR THE SHOPPER

After months of root vegetables and the 'hungry gap' of March and April, the first summer vegetables are especially welcome. Delicate spring lettuce, baby broad beans, tender young beetroot, young carrots, courgettes, globe artichokes and later in the month the first home-grown asparagus, take starring roles on the menu, their tenderness and flavour meaning

they need little in the way of preparation or cooking. Later in the month the first apricots and early gooseberries make an appearance – delicious either served simply on their own or made into puddings and desserts.

Focus: Feeding your baby and children the organic way

Pregnancy and parenthood often bring a complete change of outlook and it is a time when parents begin to question what they eat for the first time. Many parents decide that it makes more sense to feed their baby or child the organic way, and there are good reasons for this decision.

Babies and small children are growing and developing more rapidly than they will at any other time in their lives. This makes it especially important that the food you choose is good quality and highly nutritious. Babies' brains and nervous systems are growing especially rapidly at this time and as these are not yet fully formed it renders them more sensitive to poisonous residues. Although there is little hard evidence that eating foods containing pesticide residues has harmful effects on babies and young children, many parents believe that it makes sense to avoid them if at all possible.

Babies and small children have digestive systems that are programmed to absorb the maximum nutrients from food in order to meet their accelerated growth. This means they also absorb more of the toxins present in food and may, in turn, mean they are especially vulnerable to any potential pesticide-residue effects. Unlike older children and adults, their livers are still

Organic babyfood will ensure that your baby is not exposed to potentially harmful pesticide residues.

82

What the research shows

For most of their first year babies are learning how to eat and consume larger amounts of fruits and vegetables (which purée more easily) than are usually enjoyed by older children and adults. Research from the USA shows that babies and young children consume 16% of their diet as apples and oranges. The same research shows they have a less varied diet than older children and adults. They also consume more food per kilo of body weight than adults, in order to fuel their growth, at a time when many of the enzymes necessary to detoxify harmful chemicals are not yet functioning or present. In fact, research shows that children between one and five consume three times more, per unit of body weight, than adults. Other studies have suggested that their exposure to pesticides may be many times higher than average.

In the UK, in 1998, the government's working party on pesticides found residues in 16 samples (11%) of fruit- and vegetable-based, commercial babyfoods and multiple residues in 10 samples, although at levels that are not considered a threat to babies' health. Two of these samples contained five different pesticides. Fruit-based babyfoods were most likely to contain residues: 16% of fruit-based foods contained them compared with 4% of vegetable-based ones. Eighteen of the samples analysed in 1998 were organic and these contained no residues.

In May 2000 a *Which* report divulged alarming sugar levels in babyfood and only Baby Organix and the Original Fresh Baby Food Co had no added sugar in their products. Research, in the 1980s, again from the USA, suggests that the rules governing pesticide use did not go far enough in protecting babies and children against the potential risks of residues. The research speaks for itself. To avoid exposing your baby or child to pesticides, unnecessary sugar or starches, prepare your own organic food or buy organic babyfoods, prepared to the highest standards.

immature and lack the enzymes to neutralize these toxins, and their kidneys cannot excrete toxins as the organs are still maturing. Children are also more susceptible to the effects of some carcinogens – cancer-causing chemicals – because of their rapid cell turnover.

The good news is that the EU has recently set new controls on pesticide levels in babyfood and formula milks, banning the use of the most toxic pesticides on products intended for use in them and setting a maximum recommended level of 0.01 mg per kg for all other individual pesticides in the final product. It will be illegal to sell products containing residues in excess of these amounts from 1 July 2002.

Commercial babyfoods are convenient, especially when your baby is just being weaned

Healthy ingredients and lack of sugars, fillers and additives make organic babyfood a good option.

and taking relatively small quantities of food. However, many parents prefer their baby to eat mainly homemade food so he or she can become accustomed to a wider range of different tastes and textures and get used to the sort of food the family eats. Because it is impossible to set legislation for home-prepared babyfood, it is especially important to be careful that your baby or child is not exposed to high levels of pesticide residues. And, of course, the best way to do this is to choose organic fruit and vegetables.

Baby milk

The ingredients used in baby milks and follow-on milks – intended to be used for babies aged six months to a year – are tightly controlled by law. Despite this, organic formulas are becoming more popular with brands such as Baby Nat, Hipp and Eco-lac now available in supermarkets. Part of the reason for this increasing popularity is undoubtedly that using an organic formula greatly reduces the risk of finding GM products (such as soya derivatives) and ingredients such as ascorbic acid, lecithin (an emulsifier) and vegetable fats

Spring cabbage is in season now, both in the shops and in your garden.

and oils (which mimic human milk fats more closely than those in cows' milk) in the formulas. Parents are also concerned that milk from non-organic cows is used in cows' milk-based formulas that form the majority (97%) of baby milks.

Babyfoods and the GM debate

As a parent, one of your main aims in going organic is to ensure that your baby or child is not exposed to 'hidden' genetically modified ingredients. The ingredient most likely to be genetically modified in babyfoods is soya, which may be found in infant formulas in the form of soya lecithin, an emulsifying agent. Soya protein may also be present in jars, tins and packets of babyfoods. As soya is a frequent trigger for allergies, an additional concern is that the use of GM soya could increase the incidence of allergies among children.

The other ingredient of concern is maize. Made into cornflour, it is often used in jarred and tinned babyfoods to bulk them out and give them a smoother texture. A whole host of ingredients routinely found in non-organic babyfoods derive from soya and maize (see opposite for a list of other foods that may contain 'hidden' soya or its derivatives). And as these ingredients do not have to be identified as genetically modified by law, your only sure way of avoiding them is to use brands that clearly state they use only organic ingredients.

What is genetic modification?

Genetic modification (GM) involves taking genes that confer certain traits, such as insect or pesticide resistance, high yield or the ability to stay fresh longer, and copying them. These genes are then inserted into crops or animals in order to manipulate their characteristics and give them the qualities desired. While there is as yet no proof that genetic modification is dangerous, the fact is not enough is known about it or its potential effects on human health.

The long-term effects of genetically modifying fruit and vegetables, and all sorts of foods we eat, are as yet unknown.

Soya-based foods

The humble soya bean is one of the most nutritious foods available. A concentrated form of protein, it also contains phyto-oestrogens (or plant oestrogens) that it is thought may help women to avoid breast cancer. Soya beans are the basis for a whole host of different foods – soya milk, tofu, tempeh, miso – while derivatives of soya such as soya flour and soya lecithin are also widely used within the food industry. In fact it's estimated that some six out of ten processed foods contain some sort of soya derivative.

Unfortunately soya beans are one of the crops most likely to have been genetically modified. Even more worryingly, because of loopholes in labelling laws, you may not always be able to tell from reading the label that a food contains any soya at all; although UK retailers have said that where there is room for doubt they will inform the customer with a sentence such as 'This product may contain a GMO'.

Your only sure way of knowing that soya products, and other foods containing soya, do not contain genetically modified ingredients is to buy organic. Thankfully there is a growing range of organic soya products to choose from. These include a variety of milks, tofu, savouries such as tofu burgers and desserts including yogurt and ice-cream.

Foods that may contain 'hidden' soya or its derivatives

Bread and baked goods
Foodstuffs containing the emulsifier lecithin
Foods containing vegetable fat
Foods made with vegetable protein
Baby milk formulas
Babyfoods

FOR THE GROWER

With long spring days and a fair amount of sunshine, May is a busy month in the garden. There is still the risk of frost, though, especially in more northern areas, so you'll need to protect tender seedlings with cloches or fleece if the forecast changes. Depending on where you live, the first of the crops planted earlier in the year should now be ready for harvesting: lettuce, cabbage and, if you live in the south, new potatoes, calabrese and broad beans.

Focus: Crop rotation

Crop rotation is of the essence in organic farming and can usefully be transferred to your vegetable plot or allotment. It involves planting crops which need similar growing conditions and nutrition together, and growing them in a different place over a period of several years (usually three).

In the days before chemical herbicides and pesticides, crop rotation was the main way in which farmers controlled pests and diseases. It has to be said that it is less effective for pest control in a garden, as distances are smaller and pests can easily move from one area to another, and diseases can be transmitted via garden tools and shoes.

Even so, a simple crop rotation has advantages. Organic matter such as manure can be hard to come by, so, by planting crops that need a lot of feeding – such as root vegetables and bulbs – together in the same plot you only need manure that plot rather than the whole garden. Because the crops are then moved to another plot the next year the whole garden gets manured over the period of three years. (Naturally, if you can get hold of great quantities of manure you should use it on other areas of the garden!)

Crop rotation helps enhance soil fertility, a really important factor when you can't rely on artificial fertilizers to boost fertility. Instead you use organic materials and green manures. Growing the same crop in the same area of soil year after year can deplete the soil of a particular nutrient. Rotating crops enables the soil to rebuild nutrient levels. For example peas and beans (legumes) add nitrogen to the soil to help nourish the cabbages (brassicas) that you plant there the next year.

Most books on organic gardening show sample rotations. A typical one divides the garden into three, containing crops from the same plant 'family' or which have similar needs: one for 'hungry' crops such as bulbs, potatoes and other roots, and fruiting vegetables like tomatoes and squashes; a second for pod and seed vegetables such as beans, peas, sweetcorn, chard, spinach and salads; and a third for leafy green vegetables such as broccoli, cabbage and sprouts, and swedes, turnips and radishes as well. A fourth plot, which is not rotated, contains permanent crops like artichoke, asparagus, herbs and rhubarb.

TIP: GROWING UP ORGANIC

Help your children to understand the story of food and its journey from the farm to the table. A visit to a local organic farm or farmers' market is fun for all the family. You could also encourage your children to grow a few seeds of their own in a patch of the garden or in old yogurt pots.

Garden jobs for May

- Sow kidney and runner beans, cauliflowers, summer broccoli, cucumbers, lettuce, oriental greens, cress, chicory, spinach, beets, cabbages and salsify
- Plant out celery and celeriac, lettuce and runner beans that have been raised inside
- In warmer parts of the country you can transplant sweetcorn, tomatoes and peppers outside
- Cover germinating carrots with anti-carrot-fly netting
- Sow green manures such as alfalfa, buckwheat, clovers, fenugreek, lupins, mustard, *phacelia*, winter tares and trefoil
- Hoe, mulch and be on the lookout for all pests
- Look out for caterpillars on fruit. Pick off any with leaf miner larvae or mildew on and be on the alert for slugworm damage. Set pheremone traps (see p 146)
- Thin peaches, apricots and green gooseberries: if mildew appears on gooseberries, prune out worst infected shoots and water well at the roots
- Check raspberry canes for raspberry beetle, spur blight and cane midge. Thinning the young canes will allow air to circulate
- Thin grape bunches on vines: feed with manure water or comfrey tea
- Water strawberries and, if growing under cover, ventilate to allow bees access

Red beet planted in your vegetable plot adds fabulous colour to your garden as well as to your salads.

Lizzie Vann's fruity rice with chicken and apricots

This delicious homemade recipe, one of Lizzie's own favourites, is suitable for babies of 7 months plus.

Preparation time: 15 minutes
Cooking time: 25 minutes
Serves: 1

1 small organic onion, finely chopped

1 tsp organic olive oil

1 small fresh organic apricot (peeled) or two dried organic apricots, chopped into small pieces

1 tbsp raw minced organic chicken

1 tbsp organic tomato purée

1 dessertspoon organic sultanas

1 pinch each of organic rosemary, cinnamon, coriander and garlic

1 tbsp organic long-grain or basmati rice

1. Fry the onion in a teaspoon of olive oil in a frying pan.

2. Add the apricot, minced chicken, tomato purée and sultanas to the pan. Stir well.

3. Add the herbs, spices and garlic with six tablespoons of water. Bring to boil and simmer for 20 minutes.

4. In a separate pan, boil a tablespoon of long-grain or basmati rice for 20 minutes. Drain.

5. Mix half the cooked rice into the chicken mixture and reserve the rest.

6. Slightly cool the mixture then purée roughly or mash. Add reserved rice and mix well, adding extra water if necessary. Serve with puréed spinach and puréed carrots.

june

Eastbrook Farm, situated in glorious downland near the village of Bishopstone in Wiltshire, is a mixed organic enterprise. The farm is run by Helen Browning, a woman of enormous warmth and passion, who is deeply committed to spreading the organic message.

She rears pigs, cows and sheep for meat, with two dairy herds, and grows cereal and pulse crops as well as vegetables. Over the years she has become a role model for all organic farmers, including Pat Archer, and sometimes finds time in her busy schedule to give advice to Graham Harvey, Agricultural Editor of *The Archers*, on Bridge Farm storylines.

Eastbrook is a tenant farm owned by the Church of England, and Helen's father took over its management in 1950. Helen grew up here and always knew she wanted to be a farmer, so, when she graduated with a BSc from Harper Adams Agricultural College in 1986, she returned to her childhood home. When her father wanted to move to another farm, Helen, then aged 24, took over Eastbrook's management and began the farm's conversion to organic practice.

While at college Helen had been involved in a research project for the Ministry of Agriculture, Fisheries and Food (MAFF) into organic farming methods, and an assessment of the overall profitability of organic farming. She had visited intensive pig- and poultry-rearing units, and been appalled at what she had seen. The animals and birds were being raised in dreadful, overcrowded conditions, which often led farmers to becoming dependent on using antibiotics to keep them healthy. Like most people in the organic movement, Helen was convinced that an animal's welfare directly affected the quality of the food

A young piglet, allowed to run freely outside, returning to its arc.

it produced, and by 1989 she had established Eastbrook Farms Organic Meat (EFOM), rearing livestock in the best conditions possible to ensure a happy and healthy existence for the animals and the best quality, tastiest meat for her customers.

As well as caring for the welfare of her livestock, Helen cares deeply about the environment and conservation. She had been disturbed by the trend in the sixties and seventies to remove large areas of hedgerow to create vast fields that were thought to be more conducive to single-crop growing. She was unhappy about the loss of wildlife habitat and the effect on the beauty of the landscape and, thus, part of her work at Eastbrook is concerned with restoring these hedgerows and re-creating smaller fields once more. These are better suited to an organic farming system, which depends on crop and livestock rotation.

When I began to research this book, Helen was one of the first people I contacted. I first met her 10 years ago and was aware of the huge amount of energy and commitment she has for the organic message and for Eastbrook. Helen loves the farm and her animals passionately, and when I visited her in June, the countryside was looking its best.

Helen asked me what I'd like to see first and, without hesitation, I chose the pigs. Having paid a visit the previous year I knew how Helen especially loves them, and I had fallen for them too. Hundreds of pigs are raised each year in wonderful free-range conditions, on high downland pastures, and they are a marvellous sight. The British Saddleback sows are crossed with

Duroc boars and this cross produces leaner meat with excellent flavour, especially good for bacon. The 120 sows farrow twice a year, usually producing 9 or 10 piglets each time. The sows have a breeding life of about 8–10 years and farrowing takes place throughout the year, with the piglets remaining with the sows for a minimum of six weeks before they are weaned.

The pig families are a joy to behold, and watching the behaviour of the delightful little creatures as they run and play together like happy children, while their mothers graze the grass contentedly, can't fail to make you smile. Each sow has her own arc (a large semi-circular corrugated iron shelter, which is strawed down inside where the pigs are born) and paddock. These are divided from each other by electric fencing, which the tiny piglets are able to run underneath. They regularly cross over between family groups, and sometimes suckle from different sows, which is good for their immune system, but they always return to their own mothers at night.

After eight weeks the growing piglets, or weaners, move into larger arcs known as chalets with outdoor strawed runs where they stay for about 10 days. It is at this stage that the sexes are split up, owing to the over-enthusiastic behaviour of the young males, and then they move to their finishing paddocks, where they feed and play and where they will remain until they go for slaughter at around 26 weeks. The weaners are fed on a mixed diet of cereals, pulses and full-fat soya, and are given round bale silage (grass grown on the farm and cut, wrapped in layers of black polythene and stored for winter feed) when the grass is sparse – a minimum of 80% of their feed is required to be fully organic.

It is true that piglets have a short life, but you only have to see Helen's pigs to realize what a wonderful quality that life has. They run freely and, under organic rules, teeth-cutting, tail-docking and unnecessary castration are forbidden. Because organic farming depends on rotation of livestock and crops the pigs are regularly moved to fresh pastures, which is both good for the soil (as they supply it with useful nutrients) and for the pigs' diet and well-being. The love and respect shown to these pigs is a key factor to Eastbrook's success in producing meat of outstanding quality. I really didn't feel bad when I enjoyed the pork I bought from Eastbrook's farm shop, because I knew what lovely lives those pigs had led.

In paddocks near the pigs there are sheep and their lambs. Eastbrook keeps North Country Mules, which lamb to

Weeding at Eastbrook which, despite sophisticated equipment, is not hands free.

a Suffolk ram in February, and has a small flock of Hebridean ewes, which lamb in May. These are hardy sheep, ideally suited to organic farming, and their meat is lean with a lovely flavour, very good, I have been told, for long slow cooking in an Aga.

In 1997 Helen introduced a new organic vegetable enterprise to East-brook, which is managed by Roger Holden, whose brother Patrick is Director of the Soil Association. It has expanded from its original 10 acres (5 of carrots and 5 of winter cabbage) to 30 acres. A large percentage of the vegetables produced goes to supermarkets, but a lot go to businesses for box delivery schemes. The less perfect produce may end up in soup and juice processing. Last year carrots averaged yields of 15 tons per acre, and potatoes 12 tons per acre. I saw a large field of carrots and potatoes which were looking good, but Helen revealed that weeding is a constant problem with the veg crops, and needs to be controlled by employing casual labour in the summer and autumn. This need is being reduced somewhat because the farm has got a new toy – a smart new tractor, with a very sophisticated-looking piece of weeding equipment, but it appears that the job of weeding is still not a hands-free exercise!

Eastbrook has two dairy herds – the Eastbrook herd and the Cuesbrook herd – of pedigree Friesian–Holstein cows. In order to produce milk a cow has to have a calf every year. Male calves serve no purpose in a dairy herd and are not suitable beef animals either, so they are usually killed at a few days old. Cows past their prime as milkers, or who may have temperament problems that make them difficult in the milking parlour are also a problem. However, a completely new veal-calf rearing scheme was introduced to the farm in 1997, and both these problems have been solved.

Retired dairy cows make excellent surrogate mothers, and can rear up to four calves at a time until they are about six months old. A huge building has been erected and divided into separate penned areas. Here the nurse cows rear the calves until they are ready to go out to the fields with them, where they continue to raise them in the summer months. The calves do better with a mother figure than they do being fed on organic milk from an artificial teat. They are better behaved and more

Instead of weaning the young on to artificial teats, retired dairy cows act as surrogate mothers to help rear more contented calves.

Eastbrook Farms
Organic Meat shop
in the nearby village
of Shrivenham.

content. As with the pigs raised in free-range, natural conditions, the calves
and their adopted mothers make a charming sight. The meat produced is
known as 'rose' veal and has a wonderful flavour and texture, and it is hard
to imagine anything further from the dreadful images we have of sad-eyed,
frightened calves, raised in intensive calf-rearing units, than those at Eastbrook.

At one end of the large calf-rearing building lives one of the farm's beef
bulls. He is one of three from HRH The Prince of Wales's Duchy Home Farm
in Gloucestershire and is a placid, happy Aberdeen Angus. These black beasts
breed with the dairy herd to produce Eastbrook's beef and dairy heifers.

Eastbrook Farms Organic Meat began in 1989 with two large refrigerat-
ed units on the farm, where meat was butchered, and where bacon was cured
to be sold at the farm shop in nearby Shrivenham. The white-painted shop
is delightful and still going strong, situated in a terrace in the very pretty old
village. The staff are, as you would expect, knowledgeable and helpful, and
although it specializes in selling Eastbrook Farm meat, there is an excellent
range of groceries and fresh vegetables as well, so it's a very tempting place.
They have even launched a range of children's foods, 'Helen Browning's
Totally Organic Beef (and Lamb and Pork) Cakelets', to rival the plethora of
cheap, tasteless and often not very nutritious products currently enticing the
young. I bought meat for Sunday lunch and some excellent fresh vegetables.

EFOM has expanded into a flourishing business and meat is now sold by
mail order and home delivery service, too. A monthly newsletter updates
customers with seasonal offers, prices and new and interesting sausage
varieties. In 1998 Eastbrook became involved with Sainsbury's organic story
and selected stores sell exclusive ranges of their meat, bacon and sausages.
EFOM also works with other farmers in an advisory capacity, and has
contracts to visit them and discuss ideas to try to meet the hugely increased
demand for organic meat.

Eastbrook is involved in a three-year research project funded by MAFF into pig breeding, feeding and stocking systems – assessing the free-range and housing issues and feed and diets as well as ultimately, of course, cooking and taste. A new building has been adapted into four huge pig pens, with outside runs, to house pigs for the last five or six weeks of their lives. This doesn't seem to create any discomfort or behavioural restrictions for the pigs, nor does it compromise organic standards.

Tim Finney, who was in charge of Farming Programmes at BBC Pebble Mill until a few years ago, now works full time at the farm. He has recently paid two visits to Germany to investigate the possibility of Eastbrook importing organic pork for a company with whom they have close links. Such has been the growth in demand that, for the moment, there isn't enough produced in the UK to meet it. Despite the fact that most organic pigs in Germany are raised indoors, Tim was more than happy with their clean, healthy conditions, but was concerned that Soil Association standards require free-range production and so he invited the readers of Eastbrook's newsletter to comment as to whether they felt importing such pigs might be acceptable.

Eastbrook farmhouse buzzes with energy and people. Organic farming provides more employment than conventional farming, not only in the care of livestock but also in areas of research and marketing. The organic conversion of Eastbrook was undertaken slowly at first, to ensure that it worked in all practical and economic ways, and the last area of land began its conversion in 1995. The farm has flourished and expanded under Helen's management, and the business employs around 25 people, 14 of whom work on the farm direct.

One of the knock-on effects of the increased staff at Eastbrook is that the village community has grown. The school is not under threat, and the village pub enjoys huge benefits, often serving over 100 meals a week to visitors and staff. Organic Sunday lunches are available, and organic burgers and sausages are always favourites. Eastbrook has become involved with the Soil Association Farm Trail scheme, and school parties, as well as other visitors, are welcome by appointment. The farm also holds regular open days so that the public can see what organic farming means in practice.

The quality of life enjoyed by the farm's animals, together with the delight and pride all the staff obviously take in their work, is remarkable.

A visit would surely convince even the greatest cynic of the benefits of organic farming. Walking the farm trail, which includes a beautiful hidden valley, is a wonderful and calming experience. Wildlife and flowers flourish on the farm – I saw the first hare I had seen for several years, and rare wild orchids grow in the valley. Some of the staff have carried out an unofficial survey of birdlife and over 70 species have been observed. An official research project is being undertaken by the Zoology department of Oxford University to compare the bird populations on conventional and organic farms.

The Eastbrook tenancy is a three-generation one and Helen hopes that her daughter, Sophie, will one day want to take on the farm's management. Helen claims that this would leave her time to pursue other interests as well. In addition to managing Eastbrook she is current Chairperson of the Soil Association, works closely with the Ministry of Agriculture, Fisheries and Food, gives lectures and talks all over the world, takes part in tv and radio broadcasts and much more besides. For her work in the organic movement, she was deservedly awarded the OBE in the 1998 Queen's Birthday Honours. Helen Browning has remarkable energy and she once told me that because of her scientific interest she sometimes wished she had five lives so that she could have devoted one to being an agricultural scientist. When you see the amount Helen packs into one life, its daunting to think of multiplying it by five!

The beautiful hidden valley at Eastbrook where people can walk their farm trail.

practical organics

June marks the real start of summer – a season of abundance for fresh fruit and veg. There's a wide variety of fresh, local produce on offer in the stores, markets and box schemes. If you've been growing your own, it's time to begin reaping the results of your labour.

What to try in
june

Vegetables
Asparagus
Broad beans
Courgettes
French beans *(i)*
Globe artichokes
Kohlrabi
Peas
Potatoes (early)
Radishes
Salad veg
Spinach (summer)
Spring cabbage

Fruit
Apricots
Blackcurrants
Cherries
Plums
Gooseberries
Raspberries
Redcurrants
Rhubarb
Strawberries

FOR THE SHOPPER

This is a wonderful month for summer salads. Salad leaves, tomatoes, cucumbers, radishes, spring onions and herbs are all abundant. There's traditional lettuce and lots of more unusual organic leaves. Rocket, oak leaf lettuce, baby spinach leaves and even flowers like nasturtiums will all add variety and colour to salads.

Fresh young globe artichokes – simply cook and serve with olive oil and lemon or a simple hollandaise sauce – are coming into season, and the first of the courgettes, sweet young peas and baby broad beans will be ready by the end of the month. Soft summer fruit like strawberries, cherries, raspberries, redcurrants, gooseberries and, towards the end of June, apricots are plentiful, too. Herbs are thriving and can be grown in the smallest window box or windowsill pots.

Focus: Beef, pork and lamb

The public demand for ever cheaper meat products often results in intensive farming. It is fairly unlikely that non-organic sheep are farmed intensively, simply because it is not easy to farm animals that roam on hillsides, and non-organic cows are also less likely to be reared this way, too. For pigs, we are beginning to see changes and welfare improvements but, until quite recently, they have often been subject to intensive rearing. Some food experts argue that intensive rearing methods are responsible for bland, tasteless meat. By buying organically reared meat you can be sure that, whatever the animal – sheep, cow or pig – they have been allowed to range freely and have not been kept in pens and unnatural conditions.

According to the Soil Association (see p 100), 80% of pigs and almost half of all sheep and cattle are given routine antibiotics. Many doctors believe that the widespread use of antibiotics is a key cause of the increased incidence of antibiotic resistance found in humans. Many followers of an organic way of life believe that the meat from these animals is positively detrimental to human health. Indeed, many argue that, but for intensive farming, the devastating outbreak of BSE (bovine spongiform encephalopathy) which has crippled the British beef industry might never have happened. It is heartening to know that the feeding of animal proteins (thought to be the source of BSE getting into the food chain) to organically raised cattle and sheep was outlawed by the Soil Association as early as 1983 – years before the BSE outbreak – and that there have been no recorded cases of organically raised stock contracting BSE.

The organic bonus

When you buy organic meat you can be sure that what you are getting has been produced from healthy animals that have been humanely reared, in conditions that put their physical and emotional health and well-being first.

TIP: SAVING SCHEMES

If you find organic meat a bit pricey, why not get together with some friends and buy a half or whole lamb, pig or cow? This is much cheaper than buying separate meat portions and your local butcher or producer can usually be persuaded to cut the meat into joints for you.

Good, clean living conditions produce contented pigs and livestock, which means tenderer, healthier meat.

Organic farmers, like Helen Browning, often have a special interest in farming traditional breeds known for the superb flavour of their meat. Their herds are usually smaller, and animals mature slowly and naturally and graze freely outside when the weather allows. At other times they are housed in sheds or shelters with comfortable bedding (straw rather than slatted concrete, which is used on many non-organic farms), where they have plenty of room to stand up, move around, groom themselves and play within sight and sound of other animals of their own kind, or within sight and sound of humans and other farmyard animals.

Nutrition counts

Organically raised animals are bred on farms that conform to organic principles, with rotation of crops and an emphasis on harmony with nature. Sound nutrition is the cornerstone of the animals' health and vitality. Organic livestock farmers feed their animals mainly on natural, organic food-stuffs with no artificial fertilizers or pesticides. Mineral 'licks' with flavour enhancers and vita-min and mineral supplements added are banned.

Because the animals are well fed and less stressed, their immune systems are healthier, giving them more natural resistance to disease. Antibiotics and all growth promoters are banned and chemically synthesized drugs are only used where strictly necessary in critical cases – unlike in most non-organic herds. If such medicines are given, the farmer must wait three times longer than the manufacturer's usual withdrawal period before organic meat or milk can be consumed afterwards. Many organic farmers prefer to use complementary and natural therapies such as homeopathy, naturopathy, herbal medicines, even acupuncture, to treat animals wherever possible.

This concern for animal welfare extends from the beginning to the end of their lives. Even though most of us don't like to think too hard about it, the way an animal is slaughtered is important, both for minimizing suffering and maximizing the quality of the meat. Sadly, non-organically reared animals meet a miserable end. Transported vast distances before being herded into huge abattoirs, they are then often forced to wait around with a lot of other frightened animals. Stress hormones make the meat tough and tenderizing substances have to be used to counter this.

Organically reared animals must be slaughtered in an abattoir registered with an organic certification scheme. Preferably this should be local to reduce travelling stress or, if this is unavoidable, they must be allowed a period of recovery time with clean water and comfortable conditions to reduce stress before slaughter. In non-organic abattoirs organically reared livestock must be slaughtered first. The meat is clearly identified and kept separate from non-organic meat.

The cost factor

Because of increased production costs – the attention paid to animal welfare and the longer lives of organic animals – organic meat is more expensive than conventional meat. However, by and large you get what you pay for. Organic meat is much more flavoursome and you can be sure that it has come from animals who have been well cared for with all due regard for their welfare. It is worth shopping around. As with organic vegetables, small local suppliers are usually able to sell more cheaply than a supermarket or large butcher who has to bear the costs of transport and storage. But, at the end of the day, perhaps it is preferable (and healthier) to consider cutting your meat consumption a little. Eat it a few times a week and pay a little more for quality, flavour and kindness rather than eating larger quanitities of rather tasteless, mass-produced meat every day.

Where to buy organic meat?

All organic meat must be produced by farmers who are registered and certified by an authorized organic body, recognized by UKROFS (see p 6).

The facts about organically reared animals

For all organic livestock the majority of their diet should be fully organic with no artificial pesticides or food fertilizers. They must be outside whenever conditions permit and slaughtered in an organically registered abattoir.

Cows: Organically reared calves are fed whole organic milk until at least 12 weeks of age and there is no individual penning of the calves. Their food ratio is 60:40 forage/cereals as for all ruminants but they are slaughtered at between 22 and 30 months old.

Sheep: There is no use of organophosphate dips and parasites are controlled by clean grazing systems.

Pigs: Organically reared piglets are weaned later at a minimum of 6 weeks. Organic farmers do not use farrowing crates. No teeth cutting, tail docking or unnecessary castration is permitted either. Organically reared pigs are moved onto clean ground to avoid parasite build up.

Cattle from Eastbrook's Friesian–Holstein herds, fed on organic pasture, produce flavoursome meat.

Helen Browning's Eastbrook Farm is just one of a number of specialist suppliers. Other good sources are farm shops, and an increasing number of butchers are specializing in organic meat now. Many organic shops, 'alternative' supermarkets and farmers' markets in some areas sell organic meat too. Failing this it's worth asking your local butcher if he or she supplies (or would be willing to supply) organic meat and/or contacting local independent butchers who are members of the Meat and Livestock Commission's Q Guild (the Q is for quality).

Your supermarket is another source. Many major supermarkets are now offering organic meat (for example Eastbrook supplies Sainsbury's with its organic pork) although the range or choice may be narrower than it is from a specialist supplier. Supermarkets are driven by what customers want, so by asking for organic meat you will stimulate supply. If you find it hard to get organic meat locally, many organic meat producers sell by mail order. With a bit of organization and forward planning you can stock up your freezer with all sorts of organic cuts.

The Soil Association

The Soil Association, set up to promote and develop alternatives to intensive farming, is the leading charity campaigning for sustainable organic farming. It is also the main certification body setting standards for organic production – including growing methods, animal welfare, environmental criteria, processing and packaging – in the UK (see p 6).

FOR THE GROWER

With the weather hopefully hot and balmy this is one of the busiest months in the garden. You should now be harvesting home-grown crops – asparagus, broad beans, spring cabbage, peas, early potatoes, radish and spinach – and experiencing the delight of eating something you have grown. With the warm, dry weather, watering and weeding are top priorities this month.

Focus: Weeds

Gardening organically means that you can't just zap weeds with a quick spray of weedkiller. This means you need to be constantly vigilant to prevent them taking a hold. However, you may find you begin to think rather differently about weeds once you begin to garden organically: it's an old, but nevertheless true, cliché that a weed is simply a plant that's in the wrong place, and many so-called weeds add diversity and may even be beneficial. Many certainly add nutrients to your compost heap, although you should avoid putting on seeding or perennial weeds, such as dandelions, that will seed even when dying.

Friendly weeds

Poppies, for example, provide a bright splash of colour and help attract butterflies, bees and

---

Controlling weeds

There are various ways of controlling weeds without recourse to chemicals. One of the most effective is mulching, or the laying down of a layer of biodegradable material such as straw, bark, newspaper, leafmould or 'geotextiles' (you can buy this from HDRA) between plants, to prevent weed seeds germinating by depriving them of light. Mulch is put on the soil surface and different ones are appropriate for different situations. For example, newspaper is good used around the base of fruit bushes to smother weeds short term (HDRA produces a mulching leaflet, see p 189). Another control is to plant crops close together so there is less room and light for weeds. The most suitable crops for trying this out on are the fast-growing leafy ones, like spinach. Plants started in pots, trays or modules (see pp 53–5) are more mature when planted out, giving them a better chance of fighting off weeds. Finally, there really is no substitute for regular hoeing and hand weeding, although this is more successful for shallow-rooted weeds than for those with very deep or spreading roots.

---

birds. Dandelions also attract butterflies and birds, are a good source of minerals and their young leaves add a pleasantly bitter tang to salads. Nettles, too, can be friendly – they host no less than 107 different species of insects, which act as natural pest controllers, and the young leaves of nettles are a useful addition for your compost heap (being a useful source of nitrogen, which is used by the bacteria that trigger decomposition) and also make a delicious soup! Clover helps fix nitrogen in the

---

TIP: SUN POWER

Choose a dry sunny day to do your hoeing. This will ensure any weeds you dig out will shrivel up and die quickly.

ground, where it can be used by other plants later to help growth.

Having said all this, if weeds are taking valuable water, nutrients and light from your carefully nurtured fruit and vegetables, they must be dealt with. After all, the essence of gardening is to be in control and to make sure that all the plants in your garden grow in a state of harmony. There's no getting away from the fact some weeds are a real nuisance – notably theose underground creepers like ground elder, bindweed and couch grass.

Garden jobs for June

- Plant in permanent positions: Brussels sprouts, cabbages, cauliflower, celery, leeks, lettuce, outdoor tomatoes, purple sprouting broccoli and winter cabbages
- Continue sowing celery, French and runner beans, peas, pumpkins, salad vegetables such as lettuce, endive, turnips and winter greens for late crops
- Earth up potatoes
- Tie up beans
- Stop cutting asparagus and support plant with canes and string
- Cut herbs for drying and take cuttings
- Collect any seeds for plants you want to grow next year
- Hoe to expose and dry out surface weeds
- Hand weed or trowel out deeper-rooted weeds
- If weather is dry water, water, water!

June can be one of the busiest months in the garden when harvesting young vegetables and salad crops gets underway. Herbs, like this purple sage, will soon be ready to harvest and dry, and you can take cuttings now, too.

A crop of new potatoes – delicious just washed and cooked for maximum nutrition and flavour.

Organic gammon with apples and ginger

This recipe, one of Helen Browning's favourites, is really lovely at any time of year. It makes a wonderful centrepiece for a summer party with a selection of seasonal salads.

Preparation time: 30 minutes
Cooking time: approx 4 hours
Serves: 16

1 tbsp organic caster sugar
1 tbsp organic five spice powder
Rind and juice of 1 organic lemon
4 kg organic gammon joint
For the glaze:
1 x 440-g jar Chinese ginger in syrup
Juice of half 1 organic lemon
4 tbsp organic fine-cut marmalade
3 tsp organic wholegrain mustard
4 whole organic dessert apples

1. Mix together the sugar, five spice powder, rind and juice of the lemon. Place gammon in a roasting tin. Score the skin and rub in the spice mixture. Cover with foil, sealing well.

2. Cook in a pre-heated oven 180C/350F/Gas 4, allowing 55 minutes per kg, plus an extra 25 minutes.

3. Meanwhile, make the glaze. Finely chop two or three pieces of ginger from the jar and place in a small saucepan with 60 ml of ginger syrup, the lemon juice, marmalade, mustard and 45 ml of the cooking juices taken from the gammon. Bring to the boil and cook for 5 minutes or until thick and syrupy.

4. Remove the gammon from the oven and drain off and reserve any juices. Cut away the string and the skin.

5. Brush two-thirds of the glaze over the gammon. Thinly slice the apples and arrange over the glaze. If necessary secure in place with cocktail sticks. Brush remaining glaze over the sliced apples.

6. Return to oven and increase temperature to 220C/425F/Gas 7 for about 20 minutes, basting occasionally until the glaze has set and the apples have just started to brown around the edges. Remove from the oven and serve hot or cold.

july

The Prince of Wales's decision in 1985 to convert his estate to organic methods gave a huge boost to the organic movement. His passionate belief in using sustainable farming methods, and his patronage of the Soil Association and HDRA are an inspiration to all organic producers.

The Duchy of Cornwall bought Broadfield Farm near Tetbury, to add to the Highgrove estate, in 1985. When Stoke Climsland farm in Cornwall, the previous Duchy Home Farm, was handed over to Cornwall County Council to become an agricultural college, Broadfield became Duchy Home Farm's base. The Prince of Wales was keen to begin farming the estate at Highgrove, which had been his home since 1980, and the addition of Broadfield Farm's 420 acres to the existing three blocks of land was needed in order to farm it more economically. Since 1985 it has been the home of the Duchy Home Farm Manager David Wilson, his wife Caroline and their four sons.

My visit to the farm was arranged for July so that I could see the countryside at its best, with the harvest in progress. I was grateful to David Wilson for taking time out to see me at such a busy time, and before we started our tour of the Prince of Wales's farm we visited the converted barn in the farmyard which has become his office. There is a small lecture theatre here, too, where David regularly hosts talks and workshops for visitors to Duchy Home Farm. These have included conventional (and sometimes sceptical) farmers, gardeners, journalists, politicians, concerned mothers and others hungry for information about organic farming and food production, as well as the local school.

Over coffee, David told me how he became Farm Manager to the Duchy of Cornwall and

Recently weaned, black-faced, Suffolk-cross-Mule lambs.

began farming organically. He had no farming background – his father was a vicar and his mother a teacher – but from the age of two David had always loved family farm holidays. He hated being inside, was fascinated by the farm animals and the machinery, and by his own account hero-worshipped the son of the farmer on whose land they stayed. It was perhaps not surprising that he decided to make farming his career, and went to agricultural college in Berkshire.

He farmed conventionally for 13 years, during which time he managed two farms for Hill Samuel, the merchant bankers. In the early eighties many businesses (who had bought farms as an investment) were pulling out of the industry and Hill Samuel was no exception. The farms were to be sold, and David found himself looking for a job. About this time, the Prince of Wales was looking for someone to manage Duchy Home Farm and David was approached by the Prince's friend the late Sir John Higgs, a farmer and Secretary to the Duchy, through Terry Summers, who had been appointed as Farm Director when the Duchy bought the Highgrove estate in 1980. He recalls the phone call being quite mysterious, being told only that there was a client looking for a farm manager, but not who it was, and thoughts of pop and film stars ensued.

Once revealed, David was invited to meet Prince Charles and at his interview was asked if he would be prepared to try biologically sustainable farming. This was late 1984, and David hadn't really heard much about, or considered, organic farming, but he had begun to question some conventional farming methods. He was concerned about the safety of the chemicals being used, and hated the attitude of nature domination that dictated the removal of hedges and filling in of ponds. 'My parents had hated what they used to describe as "American convenience food", so I suppose I was a potential "greenie",' he told me. He and Caroline were also starting their family, which is always a turning point and a time for questioning values.

David accepted the job and, after discussions with Prince Charles and the Duchy of Cornwall, it was decided the estate should do some organic trials on part of the estate's land at Westonbirt. He recalls that there were many at the time who were unsure of the Prince's decision to go organic – people didn't want him to fail and make a fool of himself, and so they chose a well-hidden block of land away from the main road for a cautious start. the Prince's decision had been influenced by his firm environmental beliefs and by a visit to the Elm Farm Research Centre near Newbury in Berkshire in 1984. There he had met a group of leading organic farmers and been sufficiently impressed with their work that he was determined to convert his own farm at Highgrove. He felt that if the Duchy of Cornwall couldn't afford to try out organic farming, who could?

Elm Farm Research Centre (EFRC) was set up in the early 1980s and is a registered educational charity which undertakes research, development

Duchy Home Farm's contented red and white Ayrshire dairy cattle grazing their organic pasture.

The mown grass strip margin around the wheat crop makes a good weed barrier. The section near the hedge or fence is left to flower and seed, providing cover for wildlife and encouraging beneficial insects.

and educational work in the field of organic agriculture. In 1985 they set up an Organic Advisory Service to provide farmers and growers with advice on all aspects of organic farming, particularly in the area of initial conversion and planning. This has become established as the foremost authority on commercial organic farming in the UK. EFRC's contribution has been tremendous, and Duchy Home Farm, together with nearly all organic farms, rely greatly on their continuing help and advice.

Duchy Home Farm's initial trial site at Westonbirt did far better than expected. Red clover was planted to be used for silage and hay, and the crop was more successful than they'd dared to hope without the use of fertilizers. The clover was ploughed back in (it binds nitrogen from the air into the soil), and the field was planted with organic wheat. Maris Widgeon and other old varieties of wheat which grow tall are much liked by organic farmers as they tend to smother weeds. David Wilson discovered during this period that arable crops were much more resistant to disease when not treated with chemicals and nitrogen. The cautious start at Westonbirt, followed by the conversion of some of the Highgrove land, proved successful enough for the Prince of Wales to decide to convert the entire farm in 1990. The staff, all of whom had originally farmed conventionally, were in favour, and the Prince never wavered in his views. The whole farm obtained its organic symbol status in 1996.

The farm comprises 1083 acres, which are farmed organically, and in addition there are three other farms that are share-farmed for their owners by the Duchy. These total another 600 acres: all of which are now organic or in conversion. The farm is a mixture of livestock and arable, and David started my tour by taking me up the field to see one of their newer enterprises: their area for organic vegetable production. It was a glorious day – the recent dry weather had been causing them some concern, but the previous night's 17 mm of rain had come just in time, David thought – and we paused in the shade of a magnificent 300-year-old oak, which is home to a variety of wildlife, including barn owls.

Under the management of Ian Cox, the vegetable scheme has gathered momentum, and the acreage of carrots, potatoes and mixed vegetables had been increased since 1999. Spinach, chard, lettuce, turnips, sweetcorn and marrows were all flourishing and remarkably weed free, due in some part to a group of South African visitors who David told us had hand weeded the 5 acres of carrots. David's sons also supplement their pocket money by

Magnificent ash trees at the edge of the fields of vegetables, grown for the Duchy Home Farm's organic vegetable box scheme.

helping with the arduous task of hand weeding. The vegetables are grown for a vegetable box scheme co-ordinated by Ian and his wife Anne. They pack and deliver up to 100 boxes a week locally. Further expansion of the scheme is taking place with the large, newly built polytunnel, where I saw wonderful salad vegetables and herbs being grown, including some unusual varieties of delicious-looking yellow tomatoes.

The polytunnel stands at the bottom of a field where a few rare breed, traditional Gloucester cattle were grazing among the Ayrshires. The red and white dairy cows looked peaceful and contented and were soon to calve. I asked if they had a bull, but was told that they no longer did. Apparently Ayrshire bulls can be dangerous and some years previously one had almost killed Paul the herdsman.

Back at the farmyard I saw the large grain store, full of huge bins of rye. This is grown for Shipton Mill near Tetbury, which produces much of the organic flour milled in Britain, and supplies specialist bakers including Andrew Whitley at The Village Bakery in Cumbria (see September chapter). David himself has a passion for baking and tries to find time to make bread whenever he can, as he finds the process gives him enormous pleasure (he shares with Andrew Whitley a fascination for sour-dough). The farmers' market in Stroud also sells organic bread baked from flour derived from Duchy Home Farm crops.

As the farm is large and spread over three areas of land around Tetbury, we continued our tour in David's Land Rover. There were fields of oats, rye, field beans for animal feed, and the Maris Widgeon wheat, which David thought was almost ripe and ready to harvest. We drove through a beautiful ancient valley where Caroline, a keen horsewoman, often rides with her sons. To the side of the valley were fields where straw had been cut and gathered into the large round bales that then remain weatherproof for up to four years. There was alfalfa (lucerne), which would be cut and used direct for cattle feed and, David explained, 'It's invaluable when there's not much grass on the pasture, a real drought-buster.'

Unlike Ayrshire bulls, black Aberdeen Angus are more docile and as we drove through a field I admired the fine sight of a bull standing contentedly with his family of cows and calves in the shade of some trees. Some were wearing bells, which I thought made a lovely sound across the field, but David says that their neighbours don't always agree.

The weather was hot and the pigs had found some mud and were wallowing to keep cool. The outdoor organic pigs I saw were being reared

Green lanes are paths between hedgerows. Often planted to encourage birds, insects and other wildlife, they attract natural predators, such as partridges that feed on aphids, and act as useful organic pest controls.

on Duchy land by a neighbouring farmer for Duchy Original sausages and for Eastbrook Farms Organic Meat. As rotation is essential in organic farming, David told me that the following year the land where the pigs were would be used for growing wheat. The dry weather meant that the electric fencing was not working as it should have been. The current was not making a circuit, and the pigs were in danger of roaming, so David did a quick temporary repair job on the gate. Close by was a field of recently weaned lambs – Suffolk-cross-Mules with black faces – who watched us curiously as we drove through.

Throughout the farm there was evidence of vital conservation management. Over 20 acres of new woodland have been planted, as well as 10 miles of hedgerow, and David showed me where new green lanes had been formed between hedges. These provide wonderful wildlife habitats. Stone walls are being repaired and maintained, and many field ponds have been restored.

Duchy Home Farm has more than justified His Royal Highness's decision to convert to organic practice. It is flourishing and profitable and, as with all organic farms, full of future plans. Research and educational projects are ongoing, and the preservation of rare breeds is considered important. Gloucester cattle are being reared as well as Irish Moiled and French Aubrac. The herd of Hebridean sheep has reached its optimum size,

Outdoor pigs being reared for Duchy Original sausages and for Eastbrook Farms Organic Meat.

and some of the fat lambs are sold through Helen Browning for Eastbrook Farms Organic Meat. The Prince also keeps some rare Large Black pigs.

The Prince of Wales, a real countryman, regularly visits the farm and is keenly involved in its day-to-day running. He knows his staff well, and is referred to by them all as 'The Boss'. It is obvious that a great mutual respect exists between them. He is a passionately committed environmentalist and keen to promote a wider understanding of the subject. Groups are welcome by invitation to Highgrove Gardens and Duchy Home Farm to see organic farming in practice. Last July His Royal Highness offered me the opportunity to visit the gardens as well as the farm.

David Howard, Head Gardener at Highgrove, personally took me on a guided tour and we spent a glorious afternoon as he showed me the gardens. It was a very special experience which I shall never forget.

Since 1980 the Prince of Wales, with the assistance of many expert advisers, has created a series of wonderful gardens full of varied and often unexpected delights. Flowers both wild and exotic grow in magnificent profusion. Sculptures and other works of art are added surprises and blend beautifully with their natural surroundings, and I saw healthy and abundant vegetables which would be the envy of any gardener. It is all a magnificent testament to organic gardening and a whole ecological lifestyle.

I am most grateful to His Royal Highness for allowing me two memorable and inspirational visits, and to both David Howard and David Wilson for the time and information they so generously shared.

I wrote to the Prince of Wales to thank him for my visit to the garden at Highgrove and he wrote back in reply: 'I am so glad you enjoyed going round it. It has been a labour of love over the past nineteen years and all I have wanted to do is to create something that warms the heart, feeds the soul and delights the eye…'

Without doubt, he has done so.

Duchy Home Farm has its own home-brand goods, made from their organic produce, available from delicatessens and grocers as well as many of the major supermarkets nationwide.

practical organics

Another month of profusion both in the shops and in the garden. There's an almost overwhelming choice of salad ingredients and lots of other vegetables to choose from, too, while summer fruits like strawberries and raspberries are at their best.

What to try in
july

Vegetables
Broad beans
Calabrese
Courgettes
French beans *(i)*
Globe artichokes
Peas
Radishes
Salad veg
Spinach

Fruit
Apricots
Blackcurrants
Cherries
Gooseberries
Nectarines
Peaches
Plums
Raspberries
Redcurrants
Rhubarb
Strawberries

FOR THE SHOPPER

With the long, and hopefully hot, days of July you will want to spend more time outside and less trailing round the supermarket. Summer is when box schemes come into their own with fruit and veg delivered direct to your home. At this time of year, vegetables are so abundant that producers often slip in some of their surplus as a free treat. And, if you've been growing your own, you have nature's bounty literally on your doorstep.

Warm weather tends to dent the appetite for heavy food, so keep meals simple and light. Grilled or barbecued fish or meat needs only the addition of a few fresh vegetables or a salad and a few freshly dug new potatoes to make a really special meal. There is an almost overwhelming profusion at this time of year: sweet, fresh garden peas, broad beans, calabrese, tender young courgettes, spinach to name but a few. Soft fruit is still abundant, in particular strawberries. Fruit past its best can be used for preserving, or take raspberries, redcurrants and blackcurrants and encase them in some organic bread to make a classic English summer pudding, and serve with a dollop of organic cream. Gooseberries – both red and green are plentiful now – are ideal for a gooseberry fool.

Tall sweetcorn plants and pumpkins in abundance. When there's a glut of produce, organic box suppliers will often add some of their surplus to your delivery, free of charge.

The organic guarantee

Different organic certifying bodies (see p 6) have different rules but, according to Soil Association standards – possibly the most rigorous – to qualify for the label 100% organic, all ingredients of agricultural origin (such as flour) must be derived from produce (such as wheat) that has been grown and processed according to organic standards.

The food produced may contain certain ingredients of non-agricultural origin (for a full list of permitted ingredients contact the Soil Association), provided they don't pose a threat to health, and the end product must have been processed according to organic standards by a certified producer.

Where a finished product contains several ingredients, if the label is to read 'organic' 95% of the ingredients of agricultural origin must conform to organic standards. However, the product may also contain ingredients of agricultural origin (such as dried fruits, nuts, seeds, spices and herbs) that haven't been organically produced. That means if there is a failure of, for example, a mushroom crop, up to 5% may be non-organic.

Organic manufacturers are banned from using any ingredients derived from (or containing) genetically modified organisms, and they do not mix, for example, organic and non-organic wheat together. Organic cakes, biscuits and cereals must also have been prepared and produced in factories (or parts of factories) dedicated to organic foods and at least have units separated from those where non-organic products are prepared. Where organic and non-organic products are made in the same place, the organic product must have been processed first thing after machinery and implements have been thoroughly cleaned to prevent contamination from non-organic materials.

Focus: Biscuits, baked goods and cereals

Buying or growing and eating fresh, organic food and eating as little as possible processed food is the best way to ensure that you and your family eat well and stay healthy. But life would be dull without the odd slice of cake or biscuit. Baking your own goodies with organic ingredients is obviously the ideal but with our busy lives most of us rely on bought products at least sometimes. The cereals, sugars, nuts, seeds and dried fruits that are used to manufacture non-organic cereals, biscuits and baked goods are some of those most likely to have been subjected to pesticide sprays and food additives. Buying organic you can avoid these – and if that means eating fewer, but better quality, biscuits or cakes, that's better for you, too.

Sprays and additives

Conventionally grown cereal crops are some of the most heavily exposed to pesticides, fungicides, insecticides and synthetic growth-regulators. In a packet of non-organic biscuits, for instance, the grains used to make the non-organic flour (which forms a biscuit's main ingredient) is likely to have been sprayed with as many as 20 different pesticides during its time in the soil. This figure doesn't include those applied after the grain is harvested and stored to prolong its shelf life. That's not all, either, as in that same packet of biscuits you may also find a host of other nasties: sugar, more than likely from sugar beet, which is one of the crops most heavily sprayed with pesticides; oils extracted at high temperatures, which destroy or reduce their

All organic cereals, like these oats, must be grown without artificial pesticides.

mineral and vitamin content; and solvents used to make oils lighter. There may also be soya flour, which could well have been genetically modified (see p 85), plus a host of additives, flavourings and processing ingredients.

So, what do you get when you buy organic? Strictly speaking the term 'organic' refers to a method of farming in which no chemical sprays and artificial fertilizers are used. This means that, by definition, certain ingredients such as those used in processing – like raising agents designed to help cakes rise, antioxidants used to prevent fats going rancid and a number of flavourings – cannot be 'organic' simply because they haven't been farmed.

In the past various additives were combined with the processing aids which made using them in organic foods difficult. The EU directive concerned with food production has helped to make guidelines clear, stipulating that only processing aids that do not present any health risk and do not have any 'technological effect on the finished product' may be used in products labelled organic. For example, charcoal is allowed as an aid to filter out water impurities, but using it in this way has no effect on the properties or nutrition of the finished food. Processing aids are often used in mass-produced cakes, biscuits and baked goods – organic ones, too – to keep them fresh, and enable transportation and storage. However, most producers of organic cakes, biscuits and cereals are committed to good-quality food and pride themselves on using as few additional agents as possible.

FOR THE GROWER

July is another good month for the grower and you'll be kept busy watering, planting and enjoying your harvest. If you're growing tomatoes in a frame or pots, you'll be picking a handful every day. Nothing beats the fresh flavour and sense of pride you will feel as your serve them, perhaps with some organically grown cucumber or a few torn basil leaves. Support tomato stems by tying them to canes and pick out side shoots as they appear, to concentrate growth in the developing clusters. As chemical fertilizers are not used in organic gardening, apply an organic fertilizer such as liquid comfrey and/or manure and water every week to encourage healthy growth.

Good husbandry is essential in organic gardening as seasonal growing means there will sometimes be lean months. Towards the end of this month, lift onions and leave them to dry until the outer skin is dry and papery. When dry, rub off the loose skin and store the onions in a box or paper bag in a cool, dry shed or room ready for use during winter.

Focus: Disease control

Like humans, plants can be afflicted by bacteria, viruses and fungi, all of which tend to thrive in a warm, damp environment. Disease control is especially important for the organic grower because you cannot use artificial sprays and chemicals, but, as with human disease, prevention is better than cure. Use your eyes to detect when things are not as they should be and apply the basic principles of giving fresh air, avoiding over-crowding and removing the source of infection.

Avoiding diseases

Choosing disease-resistant plant varieties, growing them in rich, well-nourished soil, watering as needed and maintaining a good airflow around them will help ensure your plants grow strong and healthy. The quality of your soil is important: for example, making an acid soil more alkaline can help reduce club root, which affects crops such as calabrese.

Crop rotation, one of the mainstays of organic gardening, also minimizes the risk of

---

TIP: SUN-DRYING

A glut of tomatoes? Why not make your own sun-dried ones? Halve them, sprinkle with salt and herbs and leave them cut-side up on a wire rack in a glass frame or greenhouse to dry for 8 hours or in a warm oven set at a low heat until dry.

Spotting disease

Fungal diseases: By far the most common plant diseases. Typically they cause powdery or fluffy mould spots, causing plant tissue to die, discolouration of leaves, wilting and wet rot.

Bacterial diseases: Less common but more difficult to control. Symptoms include rot, leaf spots and cankers.

Viral diseases: The most insidious, as once a plant is infected there's no cure. The only answer is to dig up and dispose of infected plants. Symptoms include poor or distorted growth, and mottling and other patterns on leaves.

diseases. Plants of the same family tend to be susceptible to the same diseases, so by rotating them you will help prevent the build-up of soil-borne diseases.

Organic disease remedies

Once crops are planted, examine them regularly and at the first sign of any symptoms take action! Use your eyes to detect when things are not well. For more specific details of signs and symptoms check your organic gardening book (see p 190). If a plant does succumb to disease, remove the diseased material and put it into a plastic bag for disposal so disease spores are not blown on to other plants or added to the compost heap.

Where absolutely essential there are a few tried and tested products you can use to control disease. Although they are less harmful than conventional sprays they should be kept as a last resort rather than used on a regular basis. They include Bordeaux mixture – a combination of sulphate and quicklime – used to prevent the spread of disease and for treating potato blight, and sulphur dust or spray used to prevent and control mildews.

If you have a greenhouse, make sure it is well ventilated. Thin and prune plants to encourage airflow and prevent disease.

July is a busy month in the garden and you are likely to be kept occupied with jobs like staking your runner beans to support them, and harvesting all manner of home-grown produce.

Garden jobs for July

- Continue sowing chervil, dill and parsley, early spring cabbage for planting out in October, endive, French beans, green manures (alfalfa, buckwheat, clovers, fenugreek, *phacelia* and trefoil), lettuce, radish, spring greens, spring onions, swedes and turnips
- Plant out leeks
- Pinch out side shoots from tomatoes
- Support beans and peas with canes
- Harvest onions and shallots and leave them to dry off
- Cut cucumbers and pinch back shoots
- Nourish pot-grown melons and tomatoes with comfrey and/or manure water
- Harvest vegetables as they ripen. (It's especially important to harvest courgettes and beans while they are young and tender)
- Harvest herbs and dry them (see p 131)
- Pick soft fruits and prune after picking
- Tidy strawberry beds
- Continue watering in dry weather
- Don't stop weeding!

Broad bean and asparagus risotto

This delicious creamy dish contains all the fresh flavours of the garden at this time of the year. Tender, young broad beans and asparagus combine well to form the perfect summer risotto for lunch or supper. Serve with a fresh tomato and basil salad and a glass of chilled white wine.

Preparation time: 10 minutes
Cooking time: 20–30 minutes
Serves: 4

1 tbsp organic olive oil
50 g organic butter
1 organic onion, finely chopped
1 organic garlic clove, crushed
225 g organic broad beans (shelled weight), outer skins removed
1.5 litres hot vegetable stock (homemade, shop-bought or use an organic vegetable stock cube – you may need a little more or less depending on the absorption of the rice)
275 g organic risotto rice
175 g organic asparagus, trimmed
Small bunch organic parsley, roughly chopped
50 g organic parmesan cheese, grated
Seasoning, to taste
Parmesan cheese shavings, to garnish

1. Heat the oil and half the butter in a large pan until foaming. Add the onion and garlic and cook for 3 minutes until starting to soften.
2. Add the beans and a ladle of stock and cook, stirring occasionally, over a low heat for 7–8 minutes.
3. Add the rice and stir to coat in the oil. Increase heat and add another ladle of stock. Simmer, stirring occasionally, until all the liquid is absorbed. Keep adding stock a little at a time, stirring, until almost all the stock has been absorbed.
4. Blanch the asparagus in lightly salted boiling water for 2 minutes and drain well. Add to the risotto with remaining stock. Allow to simmer until liquid is absorbed and the rice is soft but with a slight bite.
5. When the rice is tender and creamy, stir in the parsley, remaining butter and parmesan cheese. Season to taste.
6. Serve garnished with parmesan shavings.

august

Hambleden Herbs are the only specialist organic dried herb company in Britain and produce a wonderful range of teas, herbs, spices, tinctures, flower waters and vinegars. The quality of these is superb and is well reflected in their now lengthy list of awards.

I first met Gaye Donaldson, who runs Hambleden Herbs and the Organic Herb Trading Company with her partner Mike Brook, in 1989 at the British Organic Farmers' Conference at the Royal Agricultural College in Cirencester. As Public Affairs Director of the Soil Association Gaye had organized the event, inviting Colin Skipp (Tony Archer) and me to make after-dinner speeches, and I remembered how kind and helpful she had been in looking after us and putting us at our ease. Keen to see her again, I braved the summer traffic on the M5 and drove to Court Farm, Gaye and Mike's lovely fifteenth-century farmhouse in Milverton, Somerset, to find out how Hambleden Herbs had come about.

They welcomed me in their flower-filled courtyard garden and on into the big farmhouse kitchen. Court Farm is a superb family house with a lovely atmosphere, and they moved here in 1994 in order to expand and develop the business. Once their five children had disappeared off to various weekend activities, and over a cool revitalizing drink, Mike explained how he came to be an organic herb grower.

While at Reading University (reading Art History) in the mid-seventies Mike became interested in environmental issues, and decided to cultivate his garden organically. At the time he lived in a tied cottage in the village of Hambleden near Henley-on-Thames, Surrey, and with a sufficiently wealthy population he was able to earn

Echinacea purpurea, used to make tinctures, is good for developing a healthy immune system and is one of the colourful herb varieties that make Hambleden's summer fields such a glorious sight.

rent money by gardening. By coincidence, one of his gardening jobs was at an alternative health centre near Henley, which, combined with getting to know a herbalist through a homeopathic hospital in Kingston, made him see the value and importance of herbs and discuss how and where they were grown.

Mike had concerns about some herb growing and production methods which involved high use of chemicals and pesticides. He was convinced that if herbs were to be used for medicinal purposes and be really healthy, they should be produced organically. So he studied the subject closely and after graduating in 1979 was keen to start growing.

By 1981 Mike was working as an art dealer, supplementing his income as a jobbing gardener, and had managed to get access to an acre of land, where he began to grow about 28 different herbs. His first harvest in 1982 was a success, and having designed and built a drying unit in a stable in the herb field, he began to supply organically grown herbs to herbalists, gaining his fully organic status in 1985. Around this time, people were beginning to look again for natural cures and consider homeopathic medicine, and demand for his herbs was good. Mike explained: 'Interest in herbal medicine, had been great in the twenties and thirties but, like interest in organic agriculture, it faded in the fifties and sixties. This was probably due to the creation of the National Health Service, which meant that people stopped looking for free herbal remedies.'

Word soon spread about the quality of Mike's herbs and as he couldn't supply all that was needed to meet demand, he began to buy organic herbs from sources he'd visited on fact-finding missions in France, Holland and America. The business became so successful that a warehouse was found in London to store the more than 200 herb varieties he was now supplying, and in 1989 he launched the Hambleden Herbs name in order to sell the country's first organic herbal products derived from the herbs.

By 1992 Mike had met Gaye and they began the search for a farm to develop the next phase of the Hambleden Herbs business. They originally wanted somewhere within an hour's drive of Bristol, where Gaye was still working for the Soil Association, but Court Farm, set in lovely Somerset countryside with its rich soil, was perfect for herb production so they bought it.

The farm had been very neglected in previous years, and both the land and the buildings needed a lot of work. The south-facing slope – now one of the herb fields – hadn't been used for 15 years and was completely over-grown with weeds and brambles, but Mike and Gaye saw the farm's potential. The old barns and cattle buildings could be converted into warehouses, offices, drying rooms and tincture-making rooms, despite their caved-in roofs and floors 2 metres deep in cow muck. It was a huge undertaking, and visiting friends thought they were mad; but over many months the rubble and muck were cleared, the buildings were pressure hosed, cleaned and restored, and the land was cleared for planting to begin. (Their pigs helped with clearing the ground, and a flock of white ducks worked wonders getting rid of slugs and snails!) Two staff were then taken on and, after the birth of their youngest daughter, Emerald, Gaye gave up her job at the Soil Association to work with Mike (and her treasured Red Devon cow herd) full time.

Court Farm is part of the Soil Association's Organic Farms Network, and has open days and educational visits for schools. They have a farm trail, where you can see organic farming in practice and visit the buildings where the herbs are dried, bulk herbs and spices are stored and tinctures made. There is an old walled garden, which is to be turned into a demonstration medicinal herb garden – rather like an old-fashioned physic garden. The walls will create a micro-climate where Mike can grow up to 400 different medicinal plants but, when I visited, the pigs Emmeline and Bonnie were residing there and looked very contented.

Harvesting marigolds on the south-facing terraced field. A cleansing, toning herb, marigolds are used in several of Hambleden's products and natural remedies.

The packing room, where huge sacks of exotic herbs and spices are re-packed into bags for shops, restaurants and mail order customers.

The herb field looks lovely, sloping gently away from the farm buildings, and has been terraced with raised beds. Clearing it from its previous state had been a painstaking operation. The brambles had to be cut down mechanically, because they couldn't use chemicals to clear the land. Large sheets of woven horticultural plastic were placed on the field in sections, and left for at least eight months, to clear the weeds. When the sheets were lifted, and the bare soil revealed, it was then rotovated by hand with beds marked out in strips, and earth shovelled up in order to form raised beds. Today, the paths between these are mulched with straw and hay, and the beds are covered with horticultural plastic, through which the herbs are planted. The herbs are grown this way as the plastic helps to suppress weeds, retain soil moisture and warm up the soil in order to bring the plants on earlier. The field is now fully organic, having undergone a two-year conversion period, and over 100 different herbs are grown, including comfrey, St John's wort, marigold, red sage, lemon balm, echinacea, sheep's sorrel, self heal and lavender. All are harvested by hand, as mechanical harvesters damage the delicate plants.

Court Farm has a large herb-drying room, but although herb growing is important and set to increase in future it in fact forms only a small part of the business. Hambleden Herbs supply over 550 different herbs and spices, under their Organic Herb Trading Company label, and about 99% of these are actually bought in. Processing and distributing these forms a major part of the business, as I saw when I visited the large storage building full of container-loads of herbs and spices from all over the world. The powerful aroma of dozens of different spices and herbs hits you as soon as you enter the building where huge sacks of exotic spices and herbs await re-packing and distribution. Hambleden provides the major trading base for organic herbs and spices in Britain and supplies manufacturers of processed foods, babyfood companies, animal feed companies, drinks manufacturers, soup-makers, cosmetics companies, major retailers and many more besides. Their distribution varies enormously and is constantly increasing as more and more companies seek organic ingredients.

It is Hambleden's bulk trading which keeps the company going financially. The sacks go to the packing room, and are divided into bags of different sizes for shops, restaurants, craft-makers and a vast range of other customers, but Mike and Gaye also run a mail order business. Their catalogue, produced under the Hambleden Herbs brand name, offers their complete range of herbs, spices, teas, tinctures, vinegars, flower waters and Christmas products in convenient-sized packets, direct to customers. Gaye told me that they welcome orders of any size, from large bulk orders to the lady who wanted only a tiny amount of wormwood for worming her cat. Their packaging is colourful and stylish and the current range of teas comes in packets much too pretty to put in the cupboard. I chose a selection of my favourites, Chamomile, Peppermint, Spice Delight and Elderflower, to take home with me, and Gaye recommended one of their new vinegars, Red Basil, which is very aromatic – excellent in Italian pasta dishes and for marinading chicken or lamb – and is, in fact, so delicious that it has been added to Hambleden's long list of successes by being commended in the 1999 Organic Food Awards.

Mike is a firm believer in the value of tinctures: liquid herbal medicines, prepared using only freshly harvested herbs, water and alcohol. They are, Mike explained, a much simpler and more immediate and effective way to take herbal remedies. A few drops of the highly concentrated tincture are mixed into a glass of water or fruit juice and are more easily and directly absorbed into your system than conventional pills and capsules. Tinctures are very simply produced without much mechanical help and are much less of a manufactured product, and Mike is pleased that his tincture-making is a relatively low-tech process involving only a mechanical cutter and the hydraulic press.

Tinctures, which Mike believes are a simple, more immediate and effective way to take herbal remedies.

Tinctures can be made using either dried or fresh herbs. Fresh herbs are valued more highly and can be processed within a very short time of picking, before they have time to deteriorate. The fresh herbs are brought in from the field and, within minutes of being cut, are soaked in a carefully balanced mixture of water and alcohol. (Both water and alcohol are needed because each extracts different plant constituents.) The mixture is then left in a dark stable environment, stirred or agitated regularly, and after four weeks is strained and left to settle before being pressed with Mike's new 19.6-ton hydraulic press and filtered. It's then bottled and labelled. At the moment they are using plastic bottles, but are not really happy about that, and are looking into finding and using glass bottles instead.

The herb goldenrod is considered beneficial for influenza, catarrh and urinary problems.

Hambleden Herbs' tincture operation is overseen by a qualified herbalist and they currently sell a range of 38 own-label tinctures to customers with a larger range available to herbalist practitioners. Mike explained that no one is permitted to make medicinal claims for their tinctures, because each separate one would require a product licence, the cost of which would be prohibitive. (For people interested in finding out more, they sell books on herbal remedies, and their newsletters also carry useful information.) Hambleden stresses that for people seeking treatment for serious medical conditions, it is essential to consult a registered medical herbalist. The tincture-making enterprise has added to Hambleden's award-winning success, and in April 1999 the new tincture range won 'Best New Product' at the Natural Products Show.

Gaye talked to me about her background and said that her mother had become involved with the esoteric movement of the sixties and always held strong 'green' views. She grew up with her mother's friends, who were prime movers in the organic movement and confessed, 'My teenage rebellions were about eating burgers and not having my astrological chart done!' After the break-up of her first marriage, and with three young children to support, she moved to Bristol to work with the people she'd known since her childhood who were now running the Soil Association. She stayed there until the move to Somerset with Mike.

'Mike's the vegetable grower,' Gaye explained, 'I'm the one in charge of the animals, and the flowers.' She keeps a small suckler herd of cows, managed to strict organic standards, and loves them dearly. We stood at the gate of their large field, which slopes uphill behind the barns where the Devon beef cattle live, and I watched as she called to them. Within a few seconds the cows, followed by their heifer calves, came running down the hill towards us in answer to her voice. She told me that when she and Mike go away, one of the female staff has to impersonate her voice or the cows won't come when they're called. She says, 'It's funny, I have no problem eating beef, but when it comes to pork and we're eating Bonnie and Emmeline's piglets that we've reared for eight weeks, we all find it very difficult.'

One of their newest arrivals is Jed, the foal of Jezebel, who belongs to Gaye's eldest daughter, Elodie. Elodie apparently spent nights in Jezebel's stable awaiting the birth and had installed a baby alarm intercom from the stable to her bedroom in order not to miss the event. In the end the mare produced Jed one night without any help. He's a beautiful foal, and clearly the family are all very proud of him. Mother and foal were a delightful sight, grazing happily with Gaye's mare Jemima in the field below the herb fields.

I lunched with the family on organic soup, Mike's delicious fresh salad, bread and cheese, and talked about their plans and aims for the future. As well as continuing to expand their range of products they hope to welcome more visitors to Hambleden Herbs by increasing the number of open days they hold, and they'd like to open a shop and café one day. The winter before I visited them the farm building next to the house was destroyed by fire, which they said was absolutely terrifying as the flames got very close to the house, but it has now been rebuilt and restored and they plan to use it as an education centre for talks and seminars. They are now the biggest employer in the village with a staff of over 30, and are set to grow as new enterprises are developed.

As I write this chapter, Christmas approaches and I am planning my mail order of teas and Christmas mulling spices. The flavours and scents will bring back memories of a beautiful summer day spent at the idyllic Court Farm. Gaye and Mike and their children, Elodie, Amelia, Hal, Jack and Emerald, are very special people. I've joined their mailing list and receive regular newsletters and product news, and I can't wait for a return visit. Next time I go I hope the shop and café will be open, and that Mike's physic garden will be flourishing. Mike remains convinced that herbs and herbal remedies must be produced organically to be truly beneficial. He feels that the public would probably be horrified to learn of the high chemical input involved in the production of many conventionally produced, supposedly healthy, herbal products. To quote their own publicity: 'The primary objective of Hambleden Herbs is to provide a sustainable supply of pure, unadulterated herbs, high in vitality and active ingredients, through a commitment to organic farming, the managed collection of wild plants and ethical trade.' As interest in organics continues to grow, Hambleden Herbs and their Organic Herb Trading Company are sure to expand and develop their award-winning products well into the twenty-first century.

Elodie, Gaye's eldest daughter, with Jed the foal born to her mare Jezebel.

practical organics

August still sees hot, sunny days and is yet another month of abundance. But the nights begin to draw in and there's a hint of autumn in the air and, with it, wonderful autumn fruits and vegetables are beginning to make their appearance.

What to try in
august

Vegetables
Beetroot
Celery
Marrow
Peas
Peppers
Radishes
Runner beans
Salad veg
Sea kale
Shallots
Spinach
Sweetcorn *(i)*
Tomatoes

Fruit
Apples
Avocados *(i)*
Berries
Citrus fruit *(i)*
Currants
Cherries
Pears *(i)*
Plums

FOR THE SHOPPER

August usually means holidays, especially if you have children, with extra catering on the agenda. Thankfully there are plenty of fruits and summer vegetables to cater for hearty appetites. Tomatoes, cucumbers and peppers are plentiful. Why not try your hand at preserving by making tomato chutney, red pepper purée or pickled cucumbers? The first marrows, runner beans and tender sweetcorn are beginning to appear now, too, along with the first root crops: baby beetroots and carrots. Choose tender young varieties and roast or steam them and serve with a knob of organic butter.

Early autumn fruits, dessert apples, pears, blackberries and plums, are coming into season now. Make the most of them in fruit fools and mousses, and enjoy the last of summer fruits such as cherries, blackcurrants and redcurrants, loganberries and gooseberries. If you are growing your own vegetables, you'll be kept on your toes harvesting crops to prevent them running to seed or growing too large and thus less tasty. If the weather is hot you'll need to pick salad vegetables first thing in the morning before they wilt.

All sorts of delicious organic products are now available. These flavoured vinegars can be mail ordered through Hambleden Herbs' catalogue.

Focus: Herbs and spices

Most of us think of herbs and spices as 'natural' and 'healthy'. But few of us are aware of just how heavily exposed to chemicals conventionally farmed herbs and spices often are. According to the 1995 Annual Report of the UK Working Party on Pesticide Residues (WPPR), pesticide residues were present in some two-thirds of herbs tested, although none exceed recommended levels. And, because many of the plants are perennials – that is they grow year after year – a single plant can be sprayed repeatedly during its growth cycle. What is more, because dried herbs are especially prone to infestation with pests, they are often fumigated with post-harvest chemicals designed to prevent infestation and stop them going mouldy. For example, ginseng, a root used widely in herbal remedies as a natural energy booster (an adaptogen, or substance that helps restore the body's equilibrium), may have been treated with powerful chemical solvents to reduce residues to acceptable levels, while many so-called herbal teas contain few real herbs at all.

Organic star anise, imported in bulk for re-packing and distribution in the UK.

Buying dried herbs and spices

Always buy recently dried herbs and spices: you can tell by their colour and the way they smell. Fresh ones have a vivid colour and have a strong aroma. Avoid them if they seem faded and/or have little aroma or smell, or, even worse, if they seem stale or mouldy. If they are, take them back to the shop. Check the sell-by and use-by dates and use them up well before.

Many experts on pesticides argue that it is not the amounts of individual residues that we are exposed to that is significant, as much as the fact that we simply don't know what the effects of being exposed to cumulative residues from a large number of different foods is. Buying organically grown herbs (or growing your own) is the only way to ensure that you are not exposed to an unwelcome chemical cocktail.

The use of chemical fertilizers encourages sappy growth, which dilutes the essential oils that give herbs their medicinal and nutritional qualities and that help protect herb plants against disease. Fortunately, an ever-growing range of organic dried herbs is now available both in supermarkets and specialist food shops and more fresh organic herbs are now appearing on the shelves, too, thanks to consumer pressure. Most of the organically grown dried herbs and spices we can buy are currently imported from other parts of the world such as South and Central America, Africa and even Russia (organic Siberian ginseng is now available!). In fact only a minute fraction of herbs consumed in the UK are certified organic and only a fraction of these are, as yet, produced in this country. This is beginning to change, though, as more herbs are being used in food, drinks, natural medicines, cosmetics and animal feeds. An increasing number of UK organic producers are now grow-ing herbs, and many organic box schemes include bunches of herbs in season. Alternatively, why not try growing your own? Herbs are easy to grow in pots and window boxes and will thrive in vir-tually any type of soil. Because organic farmers are concerned to maintain the life of the soil, org-anically grown herbs may also be more nutritious as they can absorb more nutrients from the soil. Indeed, many herbal medical practitioners argue that organically grown herbs have superior healing properties to non-organic varieties.

FOR THE GROWER

This is another busy month in the garden. As well as continuing to harvest summer vegetables, now is the time to sow seeds such as lettuce, spinach and corn salad (lamb's lettuce) for autumn harvesting and plant out winter crops such as cabbages, broccoli and leeks for harvesting in January and February. You'll also need to continue hoeing and weeding to prevent weeds taking over your plants. If you're off on holiday a neighbour will probably be willing to water your garden – in return for a few fresh organic veg!

Focus: Growing herbs

There are lots of advantages to growing herbs in your organic plot. They attract many beneficial insects and you'll always have a ready supply for your cooking. Even with the most limited outside space it is simplicity itself to grow a few herbs in a window box or pot. Herbs in your vegetable patch can be positively beneficial in terms of companion planting (see p 145). For example, if you grow sage, rosemary and thyme

Fresh and frozen herbs

Help fresh herbs stay fresh for longer by storing them in a plastic bag or box in the fridge. Remove any wilted or damaged leaves and check them regularly.

You can freeze fresh herbs, too (although these are best used chopped rather than whole as they tend to lose their firmness once defrosted). Pick your herbs and wrap them in convenient-sized portions. Doing this will give you the amount you need, rather than lots of extra which will only deteriorate before you can use it all up.

Drying and storing herbs

From July on into August is the time to harvest herbs and dry them, ready for winter. Pick a few stems, lay them in a flat container – a cardboard box or a sheet of brown paper or hesian tacked to a wooden frame is ideal – and put them somewhere warm and dry, like the airing cupboard or the warming drawer of your cooker. Turn the herbs once a day until they are dry and brittle. To store, rub them between your fingers to separate the leaves from the stalks and store in an airtight jar.

Comfrey, used by herbalists for treating cuts and grazes, and by organic gardeners as a liquid feed.

among your cabbages, they may repel the cabbage butterfly. Some herbs, however, are best kept apart because they compete: basil, for instance, is best kept away from rue and tansy; lavender, while friendly with marjoram, potatoes and thyme, dislikes lettuce, parsley and rue. Many herbs have flowers and look pretty anywhere in the garden.

Positioning your plants

Choose a well-drained, sunny spot fairly close to the kitchen so you can pop out and cut them while you are cooking. Many herbs, such as thyme and marjoram, are Mediterranean in origin and thrive best in sunny conditions and in fairly nutrient-starved soil. Mints, horseradish and bergamot prefer a far moister growing environment. You should get rid of any weeds and you may need to deep-dig the soil and perhaps add some organic compost or manure to improve soil quality. If you don't have a dedicated herb garden, plant herbs in among

your flowers in your flower beds, or in your vegetable patch or window boxes – most herbs grow perfectly happily in containers and pots. Have a look in a good gardening book for advice on where best to site your herbs.

Harvesting herbs

Regularly harvesting herbs throughout their growing season will help keep the plants compact and bushy. Try drying herbs for use in the winter (see p 131) or pick just before the herbs flower, choosing stems with young, healthy leaves, tie them in bunches and hang them in a dry place, with plenty of room for air to circulate. When they are dry you can crumble your herbs and store them in airtight, preferably dark, glass jars – the dark glass stops the light deteriorating the colour and flavour.

Garden jobs for August

- Harvest crops at regular intervals so they don't grow too big and tough
- Harvest and dry onions, shallots and garlic in a frame before storing
- Dry herbs
- Dry seeds for planting in spring
- Sow green manures
- Finish summer pruning
- Prune raspberry canes at ground level after picking the last fruit
- Pick early apples and pears. They can be prone to pests and diseases. Remove fallen leaves and dropped fruit to prevent these spreading

- Cut off strawberry leaves after picking fruit and plant out new strawberry plants
- Clear weeds, mulch with plastic or cardboard boxes
- Take cuttings of mint, thyme, sage and rosemary for planting out in January
- Support plum branches and pick ripe fruit
- Stop outdoor tomatoes from setting any more clusters by pinching out their tops
- Mulch runner beans
- Hoe between veg to prevent weeds taking hold
- Sow cabbages (spring and red), cauliflowers, corn salad, endive, lettuce (cos and butterhead), onions, radishes, spinach and turnips

Marigolds (*calendula*) are used in herbal and homeopathic remedies to soothe cuts, grazes and minor burns and scalds, as well as being used in teas and as a valuable ingredient in skin creams and oils. In the garden they can help keep pests at bay.

Warm garden salad with poached egg

Tarragon has a natural affinity for eggs. This unusual, easy-to-prepare salad, made with fresh seasonal ingredients, is ideal for lunch or a quick supper after a day in the garden. One of the glories of organic eggs is that because they are more likely to be salmonella free, it is safe to eat them soft-boiled or poached. But, if you prefer, you could substitute sliced cold chicken or poached trout and fennel.

Preparation time: 15 minutes
Cooking time: 10 minutes
Serves: 4

12–16 organic baby new potatoes
1 small organic cauliflower, cut into florets
1 bunch organic radishes, trimmed
200 g fresh shelled organic peas
2 tbsp organic white wine vinegar
4 medium organic eggs
1 tbsp Dijon mustard
2 tbsp chopped fresh organic tarragon, plus extra to garnish
150 ml organic crème fraîche
Seasoning to taste

1. Cook the potatoes in a large pan of lightly salted boiling water for 5 minutes. Place the cauliflower and radishes in a sieve and steam over the potatoes for 3 minutes. Add the peas to the potatoes, replace the sieve and steam for a further 2 minutes.
2. Meanwhile, bring a medium pan of water to the boil. Add the vinegar, lower the heat and crack in two of the eggs. Cook for 2–3 minutes until the white is set and the yolk is soft. Keep warm in hot water, while poaching the remaining eggs.
3. In a small bowl, whisk together the mustard, tarragon, crème fraîche and seasoning.
4. Drain the vegetables and season. Spoon on to 4 plates. Top each with an egg and a spoonful of sauce. Sprinkle over the extra chopped tarragon and a grind of black pepper to serve.

september

Andrew Whitley runs the award-winning Village Bakery in Melmerby, Cumbria. His years as a student of Russian and a producer in the BBC's Russian language unit are probably not the most obvious requirements for becoming one of the country's leading specialist bakers.

I have often enjoyed listening to Andrew's broadcasts on Radio 4's *The Food Programme*, so I made the spectacular journey across the Pennines to its western edge, to his attractive, converted, stone barn on Melmerby's village green – the home of The Village Bakery – in order to meet him and hear his story. I wanted to know what prompted him to abandon London, and a promising career in Russian broadcasting, in 1975 and move to a remote Pennine smallholding to make bread.

Andrew's story begins in 1967 when he and five other students visited Russia and Eastern Europe. Travelling by minibus and sponsored by, among others, Gillette, they went to soak up the language and the culture. When they ran short of money (because the official exchange rate they had planned on turned out to be something of a fiction), important decisions had to be made. They were living on five times less money than the locals but as Andrew says, 'We were determined not to give up, and so serious economies had to be made.' They survived the trip by eating bread, tomatoes, cucumbers and margarine, and were forced to barter at local markets – an invaluable practice for their language skills. The local Russian bread was worlds away from the pre-packed, sliced, white variety they were used to, and the black, sour, rye bread took some getting used to. Necessity dictated eating it, but after several weeks they found they really liked it. This experience led Andrew to understand how important bread was, not only in Russian culture but also as part of a staple diet, as it had been for him and his friends. It also planted his seeds of passion for bread and bread-making. During his years at the BBC's Bush House in London, Andrew lived in a kind of commune, and, as a practical man, he was happier growing and making things. He rented an allotment in Stoke Newington and set out to grow not only vegetables but also wheat, to make bread. If his local Gardeners' Guild were taken aback by his rather unusual allotment crop, they were even more astonished with his refusal to use pesticides to grow it.

Andrew had made radio programmes about ecological matters, and both Rachel Carson's *Silent Spring* (first published in 1963), and E.F. Schumacher's *Small is Beautiful* (published in 1973) had featured on these. *Silent Spring* was a work that was largely responsible for firing the modern environmental movement, one of the first to point the finger at the agrichemical industry, and *Small is Beautiful* warned of the dangers of large-scale intensive farming. Both works helped shape Andrew's thinking about organics.

Still in London, Andrew milled flour from the wheat he grew. He began just using a handmill but as demand for his home-milled organic flour grew, he bought himself an electric mill and began buying more wheat from Ginny Mayall's grandfather, Sam, at Pimhill in Shropshire (see March chapter, p 41-48, for the Pimhill story). He swapped his car for a bike, and told me that he was often seen cycling across London with panniers of bagged flour for his colleagues. With his long hair and beard, and wearing his Russian-style Tolstovka – linen shirts he made for himself from traditional patterns – he readily admits that he must have looked very eccentric. I worked a fair bit at Bush House for BBC World Service Drama in the early seventies, and there were quite a lot of eccentrics about in those days, so perhaps his appearance and the fact that he grew carrots in a window box outside his office wasn't much cause for surprise!

Noticing that his Russian expatriate colleagues at Bush House talked longingly of traditional Russian rye bread, and always keen for a practical

Organic wheat for the flour used in The Village Bakery's bread.

challenge, Andrew decided to have a go at making it. His colleagues loved the bread. 'They fell on it and broke it immediately, some with tears in their eyes,' Andrew told me.

By December 1975 Andrew decided to make a radical change to his life. He was climbing the career ladder at the BBC and his future looked secure, but it wasn't what he wanted. He took a big step and resigned, knowing the time was right to make the move. He was 27 and he and his wife had no children yet, so, with a spinning-wheel strapped to the roof of their recently re-acquired car, they headed north to try living a self-sufficient lifestyle.

His original intention was to grow food on the 5-acre smallholding they purchased in Melmerby, near Penrith, and become completely self-sufficient. Nearby was Little Salkeld Watermill, converted by Nick Jones, who was milling organic grain there, and when Nick casually mentioned that he wished someone local would open a bakery, Andrew stepped in. He knew from his bread-making efforts in London that he could bake a decent loaf, and that he could read and learn more about various techniques. 'There wasn't a big demand for Russian linguists in the Pennines, and I had to support myself, so I decided to become a baker,' he told me. His original plan was to rise early and bake bread in the mornings, spend the afternoons tending to the vegetables and animals on his smallholding (his first real love), and relax in quiet evenings reading Tolstoy. However, the bakery became increasingly important and demanding as its success grew, and life didn't quite work out that way!

For 18 months Andrew developed his skills in a small back room behind Nick Jones's mill. He baked bread, cakes and scones for the mill's tea room and, although it was a small beginning, it enabled him to hone his skills and create his own style. He is certain that beginning his baking career like this, slowly and without the pressures of having to produce bread in vast commercial quantities, was in many ways the reason for his subsequent success. Then, in 1977, Andrew converted the old stone barn next to his home into a bakery and restaurant. The village had an unreliable electricity supply and as wood was a cheap and renewable energy resource, unlike gas or oil, he installed a large, brick, wood-fired oven. Initially, having discovered that it was impossible to buy a wholemeal loaf in Penrith, he supplied organic wholemeal bread for local

The area around Melmerby, below the Pennine hills.

Weighing and
preparing the dough
at the bakery.

shops. Local bakers had told him that there was no demand for it, but he tapped into a market they didn't even know existed and gradually built up his repertoire of different breads and cakes for his own shop and restaurant. The business flourished, and for 14 years Andrew did most of the baking himself, getting up at 3.30 a.m. every day, and baking until early afternoon.

The smallholding provided fresh organic produce for the restaurant, run by his wife, Lis, and Andrew planted an orchard and grew vegetables, fruit and salads. They originally kept a house cow, pigs and chickens, but by 1991 Andrew began to realize that small wasn't beautiful in his flourishing business, and that it was in danger of becoming more of a hobby than a support. Big expansion was needed and so a purpose-built bakery extension with a vast French-style, wood-fired oven was installed, over which Andrew now has his office. The original stone-barn bakery now provides bread and other baked goods for the busy restaurant, which serves breakfasts, light meals and lunches every day.

Russia continues to be a strong influence in Andrew's life, and when a visiting Russian friend, Emil, invited him he couldn't resist the urge to return. Knowing this would put pressure on the rest of the baking team, Andrew justified the visit by asking Emil to set up meetings with local bakers, with a view to him researching the possibility of adding Russian types to his range of speciality breads, and in February 1990 he set off on a memorable two-week trip to Kostroma (200 miles north-east of Moscow on the Volga).

Andrew was welcomed with warmth and lavish hospitality, leading to several vodka-induced hangovers, and his passion for bread opened many Russian doors to him. One of his most valuable memories was a weekend spent in Teterinskoye, a tiny village about 20 miles from Kostroma, making rye bread at the home of an old lady called Nina. Andrew fulfilled a romantic ambition he had nurtured since his student days and slept the night on the hearth in front of the wood fire while the bread fermented there. He admits that it proved to be extremely uncomfortable, but the experience of baking bread with Nina the following day and listening to her stories of Russian village life, going back to the days of Stalin, was profoundly moving and memorable. Everywhere he went he was given bread, often accompanied by traditional family recipes, and he was most surprised when even the officer in the visa office handed him his passport with a neatly typed bread recipe tucked inside!

His two-week stay included a visit to a major bread manufacturer in Kostroma, where he was given a small piece of sourdough culture – the leavening agent for rye bread, which requires no yeast. Bread baked without yeast has a much slower fermentation process, and therefore much greater character and flavour. He refreshed the culture carefully with rye flour and water when he returned to England and it has formed the basis for the many thousands of Russian rye loaves which he now sells so successfully through specialist organic shops and some of the major supermarkets.

The success of The Village Bakery and its expansion mean that Andrew himself rarely bakes any more, except when he is test baking or running weekend bread-making courses several times a year (hugely popular with bread-makers of all skill levels). When the business needed more space, Andrew and his four children moved to Tower House in the village, as he was determined to keep The Village Bakery in Melmerby. Responsible for the creation of over 60 jobs there, it pleases him to be part of a business which keeps rural job opportunities alive, and his plans for further develop-ments will hopefully provide even more jobs within the business. The smallholding is now managed by Iain and Kate Rogerson, and it still

A variety of Andrew's freshly baked organic loaves.

Decorating cakes –
just one of the many
organic products
Andrew Whitley's
bakery produces.

provides produce for the restaurant. Andrew has plans to open up what he thinks of as an organic interpretation centre, where groups could come and learn the principles of small-scale food growing. He also hopes to extend the range of the bread-making courses and open a seminar room where company groups could attend courses in organic food production. He has plans, too, for converting an old pigsty into a sauna, as he thinks saunas ideal places for business meetings!

Recently Andrew went into partnership with Bell's Bakery, in nearby Lazonby, who wanted to go organic. Bell's have greater capacity and production experience, while The Village Bakery can provide organic expertise. Now, nearly all the bread is baked at Lazonby, and the cakes and speciality breads are produced at Melmerby, with Bell's providing transport and distributing the goods. It is, as Andrew says, a wonderful symbiosis.

Like all who are committed to organic food production principles, Andrew is greatly excited by the tremendous expansion of the market which he and many others have been striving for. He is, however, concerned that the transition of organic food into mainstream consumption happens without jeopardizing the fundamental ethics of the organic movement. He is worried that big food manufacturers have identified the term 'organic' as a marketing opportunity, and wants the public to know that it is much more than that. 'It mustn't just become another marketing category on the supermarket shelves,' he says, and he is keen to ensure that consumers fully appreciate the ethics of organic food production and its advantages to the health of the population and the planet. His plans for opening up his small-holding to visitors, and extending his bakery courses, aim to inspire and educate others about organic food production and its principles.

I spent a wonderful afternoon with Andrew, listening to his story and enjoying some of his delicious cakes. He is a fascinating and articulate man whose beliefs and passions are truly inspiring. I was interested to observe how, now divorced, he combines the role of single parent with everything else he achieves. Bringing up teenage children in a remote village provides them with a lovely environment for growing up, but creates problems, too. Family meal times have to be flexible and informal, and are rarely an experience shared by them all; and one gets used to school runs, operating a frequent taxi service and, eventually, requests to borrow car keys. Many of us can relate to this scenario and I greatly admired Andrew's ability to cope calmly and capably with family life.

As I was staying locally, I had the opportunity to see the bakery in action the following morning, and watched huge batches of The Village Bakery's award-winning chocolate brownies coming out of the oven. It goes without saying that I then added them to my shopping list when I visited The Village Bakery shop. It's a little gem, crammed with completely irresistible goodies – and wholemeal and sunflower bread, and the famous Russian Rossisky bread (inspired by the visit to Kostroma) found their way into my basket. There is a good range of cakes, biscuits, jams and drinks, soft and alcoholic, to tempt you, and Andrew operates a full mail order service, too. I am eager to return, and maybe even enrol in a bread-making course. The thought of the hands-on experience of working with dough under expert guidance is very appealing, and if I could learn to make anything a fraction as good as Andrew's bakery can, I'd be thrilled. I'd love to give it try.

The Village Bakery's restaurant where all sorts of breads and cakes are a speciality of the house.

practical organics

September, with its mists and mellow fruitfulness, marks the first month of autumn. But although the days begin to shorten, it's a terrific month both in the kitchen and the garden with a fantastic range of fresh fruit and vegetables to choose from.

What to try in
september

Vegetables
Aubergines
Beetroot
Cabbage
Cauliflower
Celery
Leeks
Marrow
Peppers
Pumpkins
Root veg: especially
   carrots. onions,
   parsnips and
   potatoes
Runner beans
Salad veg
Spinach
Sweetcorn

Fruit
Apples and pears
Berries and currants
Grapes (i)
Peaches
Plums and damsons

FOR THE SHOPPER

This is perhaps the best month of the year for abundance and choice of fruit and vegetables. Summer salad vegetables are still going strong with tomatoes, peppers, aubergines, courgettes, salad leaves and herbs like basil, as well as autumnal crops like sweetcorn, marrow and pumpkins. The first of the winter root vegetables such as potatoes, parsnips and onions, are now on sale. And there's a delicious harvest of autumn fruits such as pears, plums, damsons and blackberries.

Focus: Bread

Here in the UK we eat less bread than any other country in Europe and this is hardly surprising. In countries like Greece, Spain, France and Italy the baker is still the centre of village life and provides a constantly available variety of fresh, tasty breads. Most people in the UK, though, buy their bread mass produced from a supermarket and as a result they often get a pretty poor imitation.

Much non-organic bread is produced using the Chorleywood Process, which is a method for making mass-produced dough more quickly, using less flour. The white sliced loaf is made from flour that has many of its nutrients removed, and long before it reaches the supermarket it has been exposed to a host of chemical 'improvers' which are designed to make it cheaper to produce, improve its appearance and extend its shelf life. These improvers include bleaching agents to make the flour whiter, emulsifiers to reduce staling and improve volume, oxidants to produce larger volumes of dough and make it stretchy, and enzymes to aid fermentation. Vitamins, minerals and germ are then added to replace those stripped out of the flour by the de-naturing

process. Because many of these agents are classified and lumped together as 'processing aids' there is no mention of them on labels.

Once you try organic bread you'll never want to go back to eating the very different, rather tasteless stuff that all too often passes for bread today. Organic bread from a good organic baker is bread as it used to be: crusty, tasty and filling.

So what's the organic difference? Well, first and foremost the difference lies in the grain production. Wheat used to make organic flour has not been sprayed with artificial pesticides and chemicals and is thus free, as far as possible, of harmful residues. (Ironically non-organic wholemeal bread is more likely to contain harmful residues than white bread because pesticide residues accumulate in the bran layer, which is removed in white flour.) Organic wheat is grown as part of a holistic farming system that takes into account the whole environment including the way land and soil are used, pollution and water quality and biodiversity – preserving variety of species in plants and animals and maintaining nature's own variety by, for example, planting hedges to minimize soil erosion and provide shelter for farm animals and a habitat for wildlife. The second difference lies in the methods of bread production. Organic bakers like Andrew Whitley make bread by methods that have stood the test of time – long fermentation and baking in traditional ovens produce a good crisp crust – and they are also bound by law to avoid most of the improvers and other additives present in conventional mass-produced loaves. Organic bakers may use bread improvers but only from a restricted list of approved products.

Gingerbread, teabread and fruit cake, some of the wonderful teatime treats from The Village Bakery.

Buying organic bread

Organic bread can be made from all sorts of grains, not just wheat. With the renewed interest in organic food and healthy eating some mainstream conventional bakeries are jumping on the healthy eating bandwagon. Unfortunately, many of the loaves described as 'traditionally baked' are little more than the old flabby conventional loaf with a new label. It's a common misconception that traditional means organic – it doesn't! The best way to ensure that you get a real organic, traditional loaf is to buy from a traditional baker – or try your hand at making your own bread (see *Stollen*, p 147, which contains a dough recipe).

When choosing a loaf use your eyes, hands and nose, and read the label carefully – the fewer ingredients the better – and bear in mind that some processing aids do not have to be mentioned on the packet.

TIP: PLANNING AHEAD

Living organically means taking advantage of nature's bounty, using produce when it's available, and preparing for the lean months of winter by storing and preserving what's on offer now. This is the time of year to start loading your freezer or perhaps try your hand at the ancient art of preserving. Autumn fruits such as blackcurrants, peaches, pears and blackberries make wonderful jams, chutneys and syrups which are delicious with cold cuts of meat and bread for a winter teatime.

All sorts of organic products are now available, like these mustards and chutneys from Ryton.

FOR THE GROWER

This is the month to clear up and start preparing for the onslaught of winter. Clear away crops that have finished producing fruit or veg and order new fruit bushes for November planting. Lay out trays for storing apples and pears and remember, when choosing fruit for storing you need to examine it and choose the largest and most blemish-free items, then wrap them in paper to store successfully.

Look around your garden and protect bushes and plants from gales, which are common this month, by staking and tying. You'll be planting spring cabbages and spring lettuces, parsley and chervil for spring cropping, and lifting maincrop carrots for winter. Lettuces, spring veg and carrots may need protecting with cloches to minimize losses over the cold winter months.

Focus: Pests

Because you can't use artificial pesticides in the organic garden you will need to find other ways of controlling pests. One of the key principles of organic gardening is to encourage nature to work to your advantage. When it comes to pest control this means encouraging beneficial insects to gobble up those that are less welcome. If you've already stopped using pesticides, i.e. insecticides, fungicides and weedkillers – which kill beneficial insects as well as the pests – you'll have a head start towards creating a fully organic environment. When emergency measures must be taken, try to limit your use of pesticides to organic sprays and use them only as a last resort.

Good news!… it's best to have a slightly rambling, untidy garden to provide beneficial insects with places to hide and hibernate. Avoid bare soil by planting groundcover plants and green manures (see p 70) to deter weeds, or by covering with an organic mulch (see p 101). Leave plant material such as leaves and old stems undisturbed over the winter to provide a place for insects to hibernate away from potential predators.

Companion planting

Companion planting is about growing flowers and herbs which attract beneficial insects alongside your fruit and veg – it's one of the best ways of keeping pests down, as well as providing your garden with a riot of colour. The bright yellow flowers of fennel, for instance, attract no less than 500 different insects. Other useful flowers include Michaelmas daisies, dandelions, marigolds, thistles, yarrow, sunflowers and *artemesias* (wormwoods) as well as flowers of the *umbellifer* family – things like angelica, parsnip, chervil and parsley. Sow flowers in your vegetable patch and underneath your fruit bushes to guide beneficial insects to where you need them most.

Organic pest control

Constant vigilance is necessary to spot and deal with pests. Other techniques include:

Hoeing: Hoeing regularly between plants brings pests and insects to the surface so they can be gobbled up by birds.

Handpicking: Pick off clusters of eggs or pests such as caterpillars on cabbage leaves, etc, by hand (wear gloves if you dislike picking them up). Squash them or drown them in boiling or salted water.

Barriers: Plastic drinks bottles can be used as cloches to protect against pests. There are also various nets and meshes available in garden centres or seed catalogues that are designed for pest protection, too. Polythene barriers around carrots and small squares of carpet underlay can be used, either around plants or on soil to protect from pests.

Traps: Pheromone (sex hormone) traps hung in fruit trees attract pests such as the codling moth and the plum moth. Sticky yellow cards can also be used to trap a number of pests such as whitefly.

Organic pesticides: The main difference between organic and non-organic pesticides is that organic ones have a shorter lifespan and so don't cause residues. However, many of them are still harmful to natural predators and other beneficial insects such as ladybirds as well as pests, so it's best to keep their use to a minimum. Derris liquid or powder made from derris root is useful against a number of pests including aphids. Use pyrethrum (made from a type of chrystanthemum) against aphids and small caterpillars, and insecticidal soap (a mix of fatty acids or finely vaporized rape seed oil) against aphids, whitefly and red spider mite.

Planting up produce for The Village Bakery's restaurant in one of their polytunnels.

Garden jobs for September

- Continue sowing vegetables for spring – spring onions, radish, lettuce and cabbages
- Earth up celery and leeks
- Plant out spring cabbages
- Pick and squash caterpillars
- Take cuttings from fruit bushes
- Cut out fruited raspberry, blackberry and hybrid canes. Use their leaves to make leafmould unless they have leaf disease, in which case destroy them
- Take nets off fruit trees and bushes after picking, so birds can peck off any pests
- Harvest apples and pears and store
- Examine apple and pear trees for signs of canker and prune out
- Remove and destroy any mummified fruit, especially plums
- Net grapes to prevent birds and wasps eating the fruit
- Harvest any remaining outside tomatoes and ripen them indoors
- Sow green manures: winter tares, mustard, field beans and *phacelia*

Organic controls

Slugs: A perennial problem for organic gardeners. Discourage them by putting grit, crushed egg shells or powdered bran around plants so they cannot slither across. Midnight raids on slugs in midsummer will allow you to pick them off and drown them in boiling or salted water. Encourage birds, frogs and toads to come to your garden as they are natural slug predators and will eat them.

Aphids: Greenfly and blackfly can be especially problematic as they suck sap from plants. Their sticky secretions can encourage black sooty moulds to grow and they also enable the transmission of viral diseases. Rub any you see off plants (wash your hands well afterwards or wear gloves) and encourage natural predators – ladybirds and hoverflies – by planting marigolds.

Andrew Whitley's Stollen

This rich teabread from northern Europe can be made now and wrapped in foil until Christmas.

Preparation time: 20 minutes
Cooking time: 1 hour 10 minutes
Makes: 2 Stollen

Ferment
110 ml warm organic milk
10 g yeast
5 g organic sugar
40 g organic flour
Dough
165 g ferment from above
190 g organic flour with a pinch of salt added
20 g organic brown sugar
100 g organic butter
1 organic egg
10 ml rum or spirit of your choice (optional)
100 g organic sultanas
80 g organic raisins
70 g organic mixed peel
Marzipan
70 g ground organic almonds
40 g organic caster sugar
25 g icing sugar
$^1/_2$ organic egg, for glazing

1. Mix the ferment ingedients together and allow to stand until it has a dropping consistency.
2. Mix 165 g of the ferment mixture with all the dough ingredients except the dried fruits. Knead and let it stand for 1–2 hours until well risen.
3. Knock it back and add the dried fruit.
4. Mix marzipan ingredients together to form a firm paste suitable for rolling.
5. Divide the dough into two 390-g pieces. Mould each into a smooth oval shape. Leave, covered with a clean tea towel, to rest for a few minutes.
6. Roll each dough piece out into a rectangle about twice as long as it is wide. Divide the marzipan into two 80-g pieces and roll each into a rectangle slightly smaller than the dough. Place each marzipan piece over a dough rectangle to cover most of the surface of the dough. Roll each rectangle up like a Swiss roll and place on a baking tray with the final seam on the base of the Stollen.
7. Brush with beaten egg. Leave in a warm place to rise for an hour. When risen bake in a moderate oven (190C/375F/Gas 5–6) for 30–35 minutes.
8. Brush with melted butter. Allow to cool. Wrap in foil and store in a cool, dry place. Brush with butter every few weeks, to keep the Stollen moist, until it is eaten. To serve, sprinkle with icing sugar.

october

Craig Sams and Jo Fairley, creators of Whole Earth Foods and Green & Black's organic chocolate, have been highly influential in the organics world for many years. They have worked hard and been successful at getting their products into mainstream outlets.

Although they have now moved their enterprises to larger premises, when I went to meet them their offices were in a tightly packed building in London's Portobello Road. Jo is a real *Archers* fan, and I'm a fan, too, of theirs, so I was longing to find out how the success of Whole Earth Foods and Green & Black's chocolate came about.

Craig, born in the USA, settled in London in the sixties. As a result of a bout of hepatitis following a trip to India, he adopted a macrobiotic diet and opened a macrobiotic restaurant. A shop followed and, in 1967, he founded the company that was to become Whole Earth Foods. In 1991 he and Jo, his wife, co-founded Green & Black's organic chocolate.

Craig and Jo have always been 'green' people and Jo's interest began in the early seventies while she was still at school. Inspired by a borrowed book called *The Shopper's Guide to Saving the Planet* she wanted to do her bit. Her efforts were restricted to making her mother drive to the bottle bank to recycle glass. 'We probably wasted more energy with the petrol used getting there,' she now admits, but her good intentions also extended to acts like putting bricks in people's loo cisterns in order to save water. At school her behaviour was considered outrageously unacceptable as conservation was not, then, the important issue it has now become. Jo was punished rather than praised for her actions, and ridiculed by her school friends.

Green & Black's produce a whole range of chocolate, drinking chocolate and ice-cream, made with organic cocoa that is grown on biodiverse, environmentally friendly plantations.

Bad reactions to her early 'planet-saving' effort subdued her for a time. 'I should have joined Greenpeace,' Jo reminisced, 'but when the time came to leave school I decided to do a year's secretarial course.' She remembers her Careers Mistress saying, 'If you become so much as a girl Friday, I'll eat my hat.' When Jo confessed that she'd love to make her do just that (although as an act of kindness she might first dip it in Green & Black's chocolate), Craig gently suggested that perhaps it was a good idea not to fight old battles!

Jo went into journalism and at 23 became the youngest editor of the teenage magazine *Look Now* before being head-hunted for the job of editor for *Honey* magazine. At 30 she gave up editing to return to freelance journalism and found herself busier than ever. By the late eighties, ecological and conservation issues were emerging and being taken seriously at last and, as Jo put it, 'I could come out of the closet as a would-be planet-saver.' She wrote for *She* magazine and *The Times* on emergent green issues.

She also wrote about the many celebrities and well-known figures who were becoming involved in the green movement. When she suggested writing an article for the *Evening Standard* on Craig Sams, founder of Whole Earth Foods, she renewed an old friendship with him. They shared passionately held views on the environment and, before long, they had fallen in love and set up home together in Portobello Road.

At the time, in addition to her journalism, Jo was looking for a business venture to get involved in. Craig had been sent a sample of an experimental run of organic dark chocolate, by a French chocolate-maker who was looking for a distributor. Jo discovered a partly-eaten bar hidden among some papers on his desk and says that it took one bite of the wonderful, dark chocolate, made with 70% cocoa solids, real vanilla and no added cocoa butter, to convince her (a chocoholic!) that this was the best chocolate she had ever tasted. She was determined to set up a company to market it, because Craig wouldn't market the chocolate himself, due to his pledge not to use added sugar in his Whole Earth products. (Organic sugar, originally hard to source, is now used in the chocolate's manufacture.) He did, however, encourage Jo in her plans, knowing that she could use her marketing and PR skills, and saying, 'If you *don't* do it, you'll never know what would have happened if you had.'

Jo felt confident enough in the chocolate, and the growing market for organics, to invest £20,000 from her recently sold flat in the product. (She says she could always have eaten her way through the chocolate if the project had failed!) The hunt was then on to find a name. Ideas such as Eco-choc were rejected as sounding worthy but dull. The chocolate had to have a name that sounded classy and Jo remembered old-fashioned trusted brand names from her childhood like Callard & Bowser and Barker & Dobson. The idea of making the chocolate brand sound like a reliable old family firm appealed, and Green & Black's was chosen – Green because the chocolate was organic, and Black because of its wonderful near-black colour.

Using journalist colleagues and contacts in Craig's food distribution network, Jo sent out chocolate samples and the product launch was a newsworthy event. Journalists and food writers recognized the first organic chocolate as the great product it was, and six weeks after the launch a buyer for Sainsbury's (who'd tasted a sample) asked Jo to submit the chocolate for a product review. It was well received, and is now nationally available in Sainsbury's as well as other supermarkets.

When Jo went into the chocolate business she discovered the shocking facts about cocoa production in the Developing World. Cacao trees (yielding the cacao or cocoa pods from which chocolate is made) are sprayed with higher doses of agrichemicals than any other crop grown in the world, apart from cotton. The young trees are usually hybrids, mostly grown on big plantations, closely planted with no protective forest canopy. They are encouraged with fertilizers

An organic cocoa pod, the raw ingredient for chocolate. Non-organic cocoa crops are sprayed with the highest doses of agrichemicals (except for cotton) in the world.

Green & Black's organic chocolate has a high percentage of cocoa solids, which is what gives it its wonderful richness and flavour. It also contains less than half the sugar and fat of many established chocolate brands.

to grow too fast, making them particularly susceptible to disease. The close planting enables easy spread of disease and so farmers spray the trees with highly toxic chemicals such as lindane and DDT. The plantation workers rarely wear protective clothing, as they are usually uninformed of the risks, and work in shadeless temperatures of extreme heat. Many are women, chosen because they are small enough to work under the trees, and their unprotected contact with the chemicals has led to dreadful eye, lung and skin problems. Serious birth defects have been discovered in children born to cacao plantation workers, and now women in some South American plantations are required to be sterilized in order to get work.

Growers who supply cocoa beans to Green & Black's grow their cacao trees in a biodiverse environment, rather than in monoculture plantations. This means that the trees are interspersed with other wild trees, so that fertility and disease resistance is good and the need for fertilizers and pesticides is eliminated, and they get plenty of shade, rainfall and natural leafmould.

By 1993 the success of Green & Black's dark chocolate had led them to introduce organic milk chocolate into their range. In addition to their organic cocoa supplies from a co-operative in Togo, West Africa, they needed further sources. Having holidayed in Belize in Central America, they remembered the delicious organic chocolate drinks the local Mayan Indians made there and investigated. Sad stories ensued as they discovered that in 1987 some Mayan farmers were being offered $1.75 a pound for their cocoa and being encouraged to abandon their traditional methods of growing beans organically under the rainforest canopy alongside wild trees. Hybrid plantations had been encouraged in the hope of 'better' crops. Those farmers encouraged to do this had borrowed money to pay for the non-indigenous trees and the chemicals to ensure their growth. By 1992 the Mayans were receiving just 55 cents a pound for their cocoa, and as it was uneconomical even to harvest it at that price, much of the crop was wasted. Sadly many of those who had borrowed large sums suffered badly.

Happily, though, many farmers refused to abandon their time-honoured methods and Green & Black's was able to offer a co-operative of 350 Mayan farmers a long-term contract to produce organic cocoa beans for them. They agreed to pay a price higher than was first asked, and pay in advance so that the farmers have cash in hand as soon as they part with their product. The farmers now have long-term security and an incentive not to sell their rainforest land to intensive farmers. Their entire production is sold to Green & Black's for a price that considerably exceeds the market price for cocoa.

Once suppliers had been established, Jo and Craig contacted the Fairtrade Foundation (FtF) about putting the Fairtrade label on their chocolate. FtF is an independent certification body set up to guarantee growers throughout the world fair prices for their products. It is supported by Christian Aid, the Catholic Fund for Overseas Development (CAFOD), Oxfam, the National Federation of Women's Institutes, Traidcraft Exchange and the World Development Movement. Inspectors from FtF and the Soil Association visited the farmers in Belize and, as a result, Green & Black's Maya Gold Chocolate (a wonderful dark chocolate with orange and spices) became the first product ever to be awarded the prestigious Fairtrade Mark in 1994. It now also appears on their Milk Chocolate and their Organic Cocoa.

Green & Black's is an astonishing success story. The products have won numerous Soil Association Organic Food Awards as well as many others. Because of the way the cocoa is grown, and the fact that it contains less than half the sugar and fat of many established brands, it makes their products a wonderful (nearly) guilt-free treat!

An abundance of vegetables growing organically on Craig and Jo's allotment.

There is a growing range of organic cereals, like Whole Earth's Swiss Style Muesli, available on the market now.

Craig and Jo indulge their passion for organic growing on their 'Portobello Farm' – two roof decks. The higher terrace has compost bins and a wormery and grows an amazing amount of salad crops and herbs such as kale, radicchio, lettuce, broccoli, winter cress and parsley. On the astroturf-covered lower deck Jo grows flowers, with large pots spilling over with colourful displays. They love gardening and have a weekend retreat in Sussex where they grow all their own organic vegetables and fruit on an allotment. They admit it's hard work, but wonderful therapy after a busy week in London.

When he adopted a macrobiotic diet, it became such a formative part of Craig that he became something of a missionary with his passionate beliefs in healthy organic food. The macrobiotic principles ban sugar, animal products, refined foods and anything artificial. In the sixties he opened London's first macrobiotic restaurant, Seed, with his mother Margaret and his brother Gregory. (Greg branched off 15 years later with the famous Vege-Burger, but he had a fundamental role in the creation of the business.) Recipes from cuisines around the world were created, using organic whole grains and unusual vegetables, and they endured predictable jokes about brown rice and men in sandals. But popularity grew, and the restaurant became the haunt of celebrities like The Beatles, The Rolling Stones and Terence Stamp – they had, after all, opened in the famous Summer of Love. Although the restaurant closed in 1971, Craig's influence on the organic movement was evident, and continued, in the magazine which they produced for most of the seventies, called *Seed, the Voice of Natural Living*.

Because ingredients like brown rice and seaweed were not available elsewhere at this time, people bought direct from the restaurant. To cater for this, Craig and his family opened a shop. Other retailers began buying from them, so they began wholesaling, and this was the start of Harmony Foods, which in 1995 became Whole Earth Foods. They have become a hugely influential part of the organic food market and have a wide range of storecupboard foods available to customers nationwide. Their products are sold in supermarkets throughout the country and include peanut butter, breakfast cereals, jams, tinned goods, frozen meals, bakery products and soft drinks.

In his Foreword to Hilary Meth's *Whole Earth Cookbook*, Craig states his philosophy that 'Food is one of life's greatest pleasures – it should be enjoyed. A product that carries the Whole Earth name has to taste delicious.' Whole Earth is dedicated to producing healthy food in the firmly held belief that a natural organic diet is one of the keys to good health. They source ingredients from organic farmers throughout the world and are committed to supporting those who do not use pesticides or chemical fertilizers.

Craig, who for many years has been a council member of the Soil Association, and is its current Treasurer, was one of the first people to speak out against the risks of genetically engineered or modified foods several years ago. All products from Whole Earth and Green & Black's are guaranteed GM free. They recently withdrew their Superspread because their oil suppliers could no longer guarantee that future supplies of the soya oil would not come from genetically engineered sources. Sourcing reliable organic supplies can cause problems, and when crops fail the supermarkets, who particularly demand continuity of supplies, aren't happy. 'Reliable supplies of organic peanuts only became available about two years ago,' Craig told me. However, their delicious peanut butter, which began life in 1977, is still the UK's number two brand in terms of sales, despite efforts by competitors to push it off the shelves. 'It's hard to get in, but once you're there with a fine product, it's hard to get chucked out,' Craig remarked.

In 1999 Craig and Jo sold their controlling interest in Whole Earth Foods and Green & Black's to the team who created the New Covent Garden Soup Company. They've retained a stake, though, and will almost certainly continue to be involved with product development, but they feel that if the company is to grow it needs extra resources to develop new products, to remain in serious competition with bigger companies.

Craig believes that organics, which were still considered a fad five years ago, are now unstoppable. 'We saw what happened when the big supermarkets started taking it seriously,' he says. 'Sainsbury's went from a few to about 500 organic lines, and Waitrose increased theirs to 650, in just two years.' Big manufacturers like Heinz, Unilever and Kelloggs are now moving into organic brands, and Craig is determined that Whole Earth and Green & Black's must, as he puts it, 'Make it through to the next cut.' He believes that the backing given to the company as a result of the merger with the dynamic new team is the way to ensure that it does.

Craig and Jo on their allotment in Sussex, which they escape to at the weekends. They admit it's hard work but find it therapeutic after a busy week in London.

practical organics

There's a nip in the air this month – nights are closing in fast and there may be some early frosts – but there's still a chance of some bright sunny weather. Both in the garden and kitchen, the last of the summer vegetables are vying with the first of the winter ones.

What to try in
october

Vegetables
Aubergines
Broccoli
Brussels sprouts
Cabbages
Celery
Chard
Chicory
Leeks
Marrow
Pumpkins
Red cabbage
Root veg: especially
   onions, parsnips,
   potatoes and swede
Runner beans
Spinach
Squash, of all sorts
Sweetcorn

Fruit
Apples and pears
Blackberries
Damsons
Kiwi fruit *(i)*
Nuts

FOR THE SHOPPER

Organic salad leaves tend to be in short supply but there's a veritable feast of other vegetables to choose from. Onions, red and white cabbages, plump green leeks, shiny purple aubergines, sweetcorn, feathery fennel, the first Brussels sprouts and, of course, beautiful bright pumpkins and squashes – delicious in soups and African-style stews and even teabreads – may all appear in your organic veg box or on the shelves of your supermarket. There's also a super-abundance of fruit and nuts: apples of all kinds – perfect braised with that red cabbage or in traditional apple pies and crumbles – buttery pears and blackberries and fresh cobnuts, walnuts and chestnuts for roasting on the fire.

Focus: Chocolate, coffee and tea

It's staggering to learn that in the UK we spend more on chocolate each year than we do on fruit and frozen vegetables combined – £3.6 billion to be precise –and that this is a figure which is on the increase. If you're one of the millions who treat themselves to chocolate, there are several very good reasons to go for an organic variety.

Most popular chocolate bars are manufactured from non-organically grown cocoa beans, grown in vast plantations in West Africa, Latin America and other parts of the tropics where natural forests, wildlife habitats and biodiversity are sacrificed to the demands of monoculture (the growth of just one crop). When you buy organic chocolate you are helping to preserve the rainforests and the all-important biodiversity of a region, as well as helping to improve the life of the cocoa farmer and his

family. Organically grown cocoa beans are grown in smaller plantations where the growers plant shade trees alongside cacao trees which provide protection from the harsh sun for their workers and help maintain a healthy forest canopy and a home for insects and other wildlife. Farmers often grow other food crops to support their families, such as yams, cassava and bananas, alongside the cacao trees, maintaining a more balanced and biodiverse environment.

By buying organic you reduce your exposure – and that of the workers in cocoa plantations – to potentially harmful pesticides and fungicides, some of which may be banned for use in the UK. Cacao trees take three years to mature and are the world's most heavily sprayed food crop. Among the traces of pesticides found regularly in chocolates, even high-quality ones, is lindane, an insecticide which has in some studies been implicated in breast cancer. Organic cacao trees are grown using natural composts and pest-control methods, and without the use of artificial pesticides, fungicides and fertilizers.

Non-organic chocolates often contain hydrogenated vegetable fats rather than cocoa butter. This doesn't just mean less income for the cocoa farmers (as their products are substituted for inferior, cheaper alternatives), it also has implications for your health. Hydrogenated vegetable fat has been implicated in the development of furred arteries and heart disease, even more than saturated animal fats.

So, organic chocolate is healthier for you. But it has another advantage, too, in terms of flavour. Where taste is concerned organic chocolate is unbeatable. That's not just because it

Fairtrade

Fairtrade companies aim to cut out the middleman by buying direct from the farmers and giving them fair prices for their products. Doing this means more of the money you spend goes to the farmers, and is ploughed back into the local community to provide essential amenities like water boreholes, education and healthcare facilities. Most fairtrade companies are also committed to good farming practice – although not always organic – which pays attention to preserving the environment and to healthier working conditions.

contains a minimum of 95% organic ingredients, it's due to the fact that it has almost twice as much cocoa as a conventional bar: Green & Black's Maya Gold, for example, contains 55% cocoa solids compared with 30% or so in an average non-organic bar of dark chocolate. This makes for a much richer, darker, more chocolatey flavour. Most organic milk chocolate contains 30% or more cocoa solids compared with conventional chocolate with around 20%; and the milk used in organic chocolate comes from organic dairy farms, so you are also avoiding antibiotics and other nasties found in non-organic milk (see p 50).

Much of what has been said about cocoa applies to coffee and tea as well. Conventionally grown crops are cultivated in vast plantations and are heavily sprayed with pesticides, fungicides and artificial fertilizers. Organic coffee and tea farmers, by contrast, use natural methods of cultivation. Their emphasis is on improving soil fertility on their usually smaller plantations, rather than relying on artificial fertilizers, and employing natural methods of pest control.

Store cupboard staples

Part of the joy of eating organic is freshness, but there are times when, if tired or rushed, we reach for the store cupboard, chill cabinet or freezer. However, those jars, cans, packets and ready-made meals can be organic and as such will not be packed with artificial additives and flavourings.

Pesticides are remarkably resistant to processing and pesticide residues are regularly found in processed foods. Buying organic means you can be sure the foods you eat regularly are pesticide free. It also guarantees they are GM free and have been produced and prepared according to organic standards. The main ingredients must be organically grown, and only naturally derived additives and processing aids are allowed (these are only added where strictly necessary for the production process). Most organic foods are also low in other unhealthy products like sugar, salt and hydrogenated fats, though organic doesn't automatically equal low fat and sugar, so check the label before you buy.

Organic pasta is a great store cupboard stand-by.

Store cupboard ideas

The range of organic store cupboard food now available is growing, virtually daily, with more products coming on to the market all the time. This list gives you an idea of the range of items available, with some of the manufacturers' names to help you when making enquiries at your nearest shop. It's also worth checking out supermarkets' own brand products, which are usually good value.

Babyfoods: Look out for Baby Organix, Hipp and Kallo for rusks.

Beverages: Organic coffee is made by Equal Exchange, Café Buenaventura, Mount Hagen, Natura, Percol and Café Direct. For tea look for Clipper, Equal Exchange, Hampstead Tea and Coffee, Twinings or Traidcraft. For herbal teas try Hambleden Herbs, Kitchen Garden and Piramide, and for hot chocolate and cocoa try Green & Black's, Equal Exchange and Hambedon Herbs. For juices and cordials try Sunland, Aspalls, Libby's, Santa Cruz, Belvoir, Rocks, Whole Earth and Duchy Orginals.

Biscuits and confectionery: Duchy Originals, Doves Farm, The Village Bakery, Kallo, Courtney's Stamp Collection and The Organic Fudge Company can help on this score.

Bread and cakes: Shipton Mill, Allinson, Doves Farm, Cranks, Stamp Collection and The Village Bakery all make a variety of products.

Breakfast cereals: Try Whole Earth, Jordans, Mornflake for porridge, Doves Farm, Nature's Path or Pertwood Organics.

Crisps and snacks: Meridian, Country Organic, Santa Cruz, Crucial and Trafo all produce organic savoury treats. Discovery Foods make tortillas.

Frozen foods: Look out for Whole Earth, ODC organic and supermarket own brands, Goodlife vegetable burgers, Simply Organic for pizza, Shearway for organic raspberries, Rocombe and Yeo Valley for ice-creams and frozen yogurts.

Store a variety of organic dried fruits and nuts for snacking on – they keep really well.

Jams and preserves: Duchy Originals and Whole Earth make a variety of these and Citadelle makes a delicious organic maple syrup.

Oils, vinegars and mayonnaise: Meridian, Aspall, Hambleden Herbs or Simply Delicious.

Pasta, pulses and grains: Country Harvest, Meridian, The Noodle Company, Just Wholefoods, Suma Wholefoods, Whole Earth and Watermill have a range of pulses and pastas.

Stock cubes, sauces and seasonings: Kallo produce stock cubes and liquid seasoning, Joubère make fresh organic stocks, Go Organic and Tideford supply sauces, and Meridian makes tomato ketchup.

Vegetables and soups: Try Biona, Bionova, Organic Valley or Suma for canned pulses; Bionova, Campo, Just Wholefoods, Organic Valley and Suma for canned vegetables. Whole Earth produce sweetcorn and the most delicious baked beans. Hawkwood, Go Organic and Seeds of Change all make canned soups. Alternatively try New Covent Garden, Joubère and Tideford for fresh, chilled soups.

FOR THE GROWER

In October you'll still be clearing up in readiness for winter. In conventional gardens it's the time of year for burning leaves. However, by and large, bonfires are discouraged in organic gardens in favour of recycling. If you have diseased, virus-ridden material, though, you can dry it out and burn it on a quick hot bonfire then put the ash on your compost heap. If you have a patio and no room for a compost heap, you might be able to find a local small-scale composting plant where you can take garden waste for composting.

Focus: Leafmould

Autumn leaves, the bane of a conventional gardener's life, are the organic gardener's friend. They break down over the course of two or three years to form a superb soil-conditioner.

As leaves fall, run the mower over them with the box off and leave them on the lawn to dis-appear. If you have lots of fallen leaves, rake them up after the rain so they don't fly around or mow them into the grass box. Choose leaves from dec-iduous trees and shrubs – not conifers or other evergreens – and avoid any that appear dis-eased such as rose leaves with blackspot. When you have col-lected the leaves, pile them all into a container – you can buy leafmould composters from Chase's or HDRA's *Organic Garden-ing Catalogues* (see pp 189–90) – or a

(see pp 189–90)

> ### TIP: VEGETABLE STORAGE
>
> Most vegetables keep better if you store them with the dirt clinging to them. Store in a sack in a cool, dry, airy, frost-free place such as an unheated room in the house, garden shed or garage. To make life easier for yourself, separate different veg into different sacks or strong (but not plastic) bags and label them.

black plastic rubbish bag loosely tied will do fine. Water any dry leaves well, and leave for two or three years. Dig the resulting dark, friable mixture into your soil to condition it. You can hasten the rotting process by using a liquid accelerator such as Biotal for Leaves, also available from catalogues.

Pumpkins and squashes are abundant at this time of the year.

Garden jobs for October

- Sow broad beans, cress and lettuce under cover
- Plant cabbage, celery, lettuce, spring greens, garlic and onion sets, and strawberries
- Cut down asparagus stalks to prevent asparagus beetle making a home there
- Protect winter cauliflowers, parsley, late lettuce and broccoli from frost
- Sow green manures – grazing rye and field beans
- Make leafmould with healthy leaves, destroy any leaves that look unhealthy
- Order fruit trees and bushes and prepare ground ready for planting them and weed around established ones
- Pick autumn-fruiting strawberries
- Finish picking apples and pears and store those that are unblemished
- Apply greasebands to trees and stakes
- Cut out and destroy diseased wood
- Remove mulch and hoe round raspberry canes to expose overwintering pests

Chocolate baked ricotta

Try this rich chocolate pudding with poached, organically grown plums and custard.

Preparation time: 15 minutes, plus cooling
Cooking time: 25 minutes
Serves: 8

For the poached plums
100 g organic caster sugar
300 ml sweet organic white wine
1 organic vanilla pod, split
6 ripe organic plums
For the baked ricotta
250 g plain organic chocolate
500 g organic ricotta cheese
2 medium organic egg whites, lightly beaten
1 tsp organic cinnamon
300 ml organic cream, whipped, to serve
Organic cocoa powder to dust

1. Preheat the oven to 200C/400F/Gas 6. Oil and line the base and sides of a 25 x 11 x 8-cm loaf tin with greaseproof paper.
2. Place the sugar, wine, vanilla pod and 150 ml water in a large pan and stir over a low heat until the sugar has completely dissolved. Add the plums, bring to the boil and simmer for 5 minutes or until just tender. Leave to cool.
3. Meanwhile, melt the chocolate in a bowl set over a pan of simmering water, making sure the bottom of the bowl doesn't touch the water. Remove from the heat and allow to cool slightly.
4. In a large bowl beat together the ricotta, melted chocolate, egg whites and cinnamon until well combined. Spoon into the prepared tin and level the surface with the back of a wet spoon.
5. Bake for 25 minutes until firm to the touch. Allow to cool completely. Turn out and remove the greaseproof paper.
6. To serve, cut the loaf into fingers and arrange on plates. Top with the poached plums and whipped cream. Dust lightly with a little cocoa powder.

To freeze: Make the pudding up to the end of step 3. Remove it from the tin, but don't remove the greaseproof paper. Allow to cool completely. Overwrap with foil and freeze for up to 1 month. Defrost thoroughly before serving. The plums don't freeze well, so cook these on the day of serving.

november

Andrew Dennis from Kirton, in the Lincolnshire fens, converted Woodlands to an organic farm in 1996. His family have farmed in the area for four generations and, although Woodlands is principally arable, Andrew's flagship enterprise is organic turkeys.

With Christmas approaching I was intrigued to discover more about this relatively recent convert to organic practices and his turkeys, so I made my way to the fens. The fenland countryside is one of flat, wide open spaces. It's predominantly a farming area and I drove for miles past huge fields of vegetables. There seemed to be few hedges and trees to break up the landscape and, compared to Warwickshire (where I live), I found the countryside somewhat bleak, but could see why people are captivated by the amazing light and skyscapes here.

A warm welcome and the tempting smell of roasting turkey greeted me as Andrew ushered me into his kitchen at Dean's Farmhouse – the Georgian house on the farm which is his home. 'I'm not really a very good cook,' he confessed, 'but I felt I had to give you a taste of my turkey!' Andrew is a quiet and sensitive man, and was born and brought up on the family property at Stenigot in the Lincolnshire Wolds, where his father and his brother David still farm. He is a countryman who loves the land where he was raised and is passionate about farming the organic way.

'When I began to convert Woodlands Farm four or five years ago, to be quite honest, people thought I was a bit loopy,' Andrew told me. His farm is in the midst of a huge conventional farming area, where organic farming is rare. 'Because it is a man-made environment, I guess people round here have become used to controlling it, and that doesn't mate easily with the organic philosophy,' he explained. Going organic lost him quite a few of his staff, as they didn't believe the farm could survive the reduction in output during the two-year conversion. He found that period somewhat frustrating, and realized that he could accelerate the process because he already had a small amount of land that had been taken out of production (set-aside land) and, not having been farmed, was thus chemical free. This allowed it to gain its organic status more quickly and he could begin his turkey enterprise

Andrew told me that turkeys are often reared indoors, in horribly over-crowded conditions, which means relying heavily on the use of antibiotics to curb the spread of disease. The birds end up in appalling factory abattoirs, hung upside down on long lines before they are killed in sight of each other. 'They are treated like objects, with very little respect. I wanted to prove that it can be done another way,' he said.

During our delicious lunch, Andrew told me his family story: how his great-grandfather, William Dennis, son of a farm labourer, left his boyhood Lincolnshire village of Horsington, and walked to the rich farming area in the south of the county to find his fortune in the 1870s. Working hard for a potato merchant, who lived at Kirton House, near Boston, he was a self-educated man interested in potato growing and land drainage (a crucial part of fenland farming). He quickly became successful and before long bought his own land to farm for himself. Buying up fields in the area, he eventually formed the Kirton property that exists today. With five sons and three daughters, the thriving business of W. Dennis & Sons (which trades today from Kirton House) was established, and various sons ran the different enterprises – farming, marketing and wholesaling in Covent Garden Market. Andrew has his great-grand-father's diaries and journals and says you can tell that he was a great philanthropist and a man of quality. He was also very successful, and when he died in 1924 the family business had interests in London, the Channel Islands and Canada.

After William's death, the business passed to Andrew's grandfather Frank, then to his father Peter Kirton Dennis. Although both practised highly success-ful farming using scientific methods, they cared greatly for the countryside. His father, in particular, is a great conservationist and in the 1950s – a time when it wasn't a fashionable thing to do – he planted trees at Stenigot in the Lincolnshire wolds, fitting them with nesting boxes and understanding that commercial farming had to take heed of the needs of the natural world.

Discing the fields before ploughing ensures that the green manures – important soil fertilizers for organic farmers – are turned into the soil.

Andrew describes Stenigot as the loveliest of places. A mixed arable farm with a breeding flock of sheep, set among hills with wonderful old pasture, parkland, lakes, and fields growing wheat, sugar beet and vegetables. Andrew's certain that childhood, in a place he so loved, shaped his early thoughts of one day farming organically. He's been encouraged by his father, who, unlike many in the farming community, envisages farming becoming more of an art form and less of a science. Whereas in scientific farming the farmer abnegates his responsibility to the land by using chemicals, Andrew believes it's much more rewarding to reassume that responsibility, and abandon their use.

Despite his love for the land, Andrew didn't immediately go into the family business. He read English and History at university and 'gravitated more towards literature and philosophy at that time,' he says. He lived in London after graduating, reading, studying and writing about environmental matters, and spent some time travelling before he eventually returned to Lincolnshire. The family have diverse and artistic talents: Andrew loves

Weighing a turkey to make the selection for the Thanksgiving and Christmas markets.

poetry and music; his brother David (who farms organically at Stenigot) is a fine painter; and his other brothers, John and Henry, are publisher and hotelier respectively.

In 1985 an opportunity arose for Andrew to come back to the farm at Kirton and he felt he had to either seize the chance then or forget about farming as a career. He didn't have the farming skills of many of the other young farmers in the district, who had mostly been to agricultural college instead of university, and so he had to learn these from the excellent farm management team then in place. He knew his heart wasn't really in conventional farming and that he wanted to farm organically. He also knew that the timing had to be right for it to succeed and that he didn't have the confidence or expertise to begin his conversion straight away. So his early farming years were spent waiting.

By 1996, developments both in the political and the farming worlds convinced Andrew that the time had come to begin his conversion. The public had started to question conventional farming methods, and there was much anxiety over the scandals of BSE, E. coli and salmonella, as well as concern over the use of lindane, organophosphates and other agrichemicals. His friend and neighbour, Pam Bowers, who had been farming organically for many years and written a book on the subject (published by Andrew's brother), was a great inspiration and encouraged him, too. (She was a fellow lunch guest, a remarkable woman, who now farms her 40 acres on her own.)

Andrew sought advice from the Organic Advisory Service at Elm Farm Research Centre, near Newbury, who provided him with two free visits and an Organic Management Plan. He also registered with the Soil Association and, because it was more affordable, decided the conversion for Woodlands Farm should be phased over a number of years, rather than converting all 1700 acres at once. He plans to have the whole farm organic by the year 2003.

The farm worked closely with Elm Farm Research Centre, and also took advice from HDRA. The first conversion fields were planted with a two-year combined grass and clover ley. The cutting and mulching of the clover helps improve soil structure and provides fertility for the following crop, and Andrew cut and mulched eight times a year. He conducted vegetable trials with varying degrees of success, and knows now he shouldn't have attempted cauliflowers or broccoli without building up adequate fertility. He learnt to plant green manures (see p 70), with vetch grown, cut and ploughed back into the soil before potatoes were sown, and mustard before beetroot.

To farm his organic turkeys, Andrew converted disused farm buildings at Woodlands Farm and planted the paddocks with fruit trees and osiers (willow trees), as the turkey is naturally a woodland bird. The farm logo is OBO – the turkeys are the traditional Organic Bronze Originals – and I saw that the flock was raised in three small groups of around 180 birds in each as this helps to reduce the risk of disease. The birds run free in their paddocks and return to the barns at night. They tend to stay inside on windy days, too, because they have large ears and are very sensitive to noise and wind. I noticed some were outside the paddocks and Andrew explained that they do sometimes fly out because their wings aren't clipped, but they invariably return. I was intrigued to note that they came to Andrew's call.

Most of the turkeys are produced from the farm's own breeding stock and Andrew has 40 breeding hens at any one time, with four stags (male turkeys). He keeps 20 of the best hens for breeding each year, and broody hens are allowed to sit on clutches of about 15 eggs at any one time.

One group of birds has a paddock divided by a dyke, so a bridge has been built and the turkeys can cross to the trees, which provide a necessary windbreak and shelter in the summer. When we crossed over to see the larger, older birds and breeding stock, we were followed by a big group of smaller, younger

birds who looked quite funny as they trotted across in formation. They watched us for a few moments, then all turned round and re-crossed the bridge. I asked Andrew if we or the older birds had intimidated them, but he said that they were probably just bored with our company, being rude, and felt like going back home! I'd never really thought of turkeys as having personalities before, but Andrew's Norfolk Bronze and Norfolk Blacks do seem to.

The Norfolk is the breed closest in relation to the wild turkey and has a good gamey flavour. They vary in size from the smallest, at about 3.5 kg, up to the very largest at about 12 kg. Andrew's turkeys have space and freedom in a lovely environment and, as he says, 'I suppose they're really spoilt rotten.' If they become ill, the birds are isolated, but antibiotics are only used if it is absolutely essential to prevent suffering. Problems can include arthritis and blackhead, but last year they needed no medicine at all. They are naturally long-lived birds and some of Andrew's breeding stock are nine years old.

Passionate that slaughtering is carried out humanely, Andrew has his turkeys killed individually at the farm. This avoids unnecessary and traumatic travel for the birds. Andrew supervises this operation himself and although he admits it is impractical, he knows it is much kinder to the turkeys.

Displaying turkeys, roaming and enjoying their natural woodland environment.

Woodlands Farm produced 500 birds in 1999, supplying turkeys to East-brook Farms Organic Meat, as well as to local customers. They run a vegetable delivery box scheme offering organic produce like potatoes, carrots, onions, Brussels sprouts, parsnips and cabbages grown at Woodlands and Stenigot.

Turkeys farmed organically are necessarily more expensive than conventionally produced ones. Having seen the quality of life they enjoy, and tasted the flavour, I wouldn't hesitate to pay the price for such quality meat. Non-organic turkey is often sold at absurdly unrealistic prices as a loss leader – i.e. shops sell it cheaply and absorb the financial loss to let customers feel they are getting a bargain, so they spend more on other goods. I've made the mistake of buying a cheap, non-organic turkey… never again! If it can't be organic, I make sure the turkey is at least free-range, as no amount of cranberry sauce or chestnut stuffing can give flavour to a factory-farmed bird which has endured dirty, cramped conditions. It was interesting that Andrew cooked his turkey – fresh not frozen – very simply, with only the addition of his fresh organic vegetables, and it was full of flavour and delicious.

Andrew is patiently continuing his organic conversion and has future plans. He has dug a lake for irrigating his fields and is planting hedgerows. One day he'd like to create an education centre at the farm, and host organic events, too. I truly wish Andrew every success. He has stuck to his resolution in an area not organically friendly, and I hope by the time the farm is fully organic his doubters will have been silenced by his success.

Turkeys crossing the bridge, over the dyke, from one field to another.

practical organics

Winter is setting in. The days are short, the nights long and dark. There may be frosts and although the garden looks tired, now is the time to start planting for spring. In the kitchen, veg like Savoy and red cabbages and purple sprouting broccoli are ousting salad leaves.

What to try in
november

Vegetables
Beans *(i)*
Broccoli
Brussels sprouts
Cabbages
Carrots
Cauliflower
Celeriac
Celery
Chicory
Jerusalem artichokes
Leeks
Parsnips
Radiccio
Rocket
Spinach

Fruit
Citrus fruit: *(all i)*
  especially clemen-
  tines, satsumas
  and tangerines
Cranberries *(i)*
Grapes *(i)*
Mangoes *(i)*
Melon *(i)*

FOR THE SHOPPER

As you'll know by now organic living means eating with the seasons. Once you do this you start to appreciate how nature provides just the right food for the time of year. For example, root vegetables like carrots, potatoes, parsnips (best after a frost, as are Brussels sprouts) and celeriac are now coming into their own and are perfect for warming stews and casseroles to fend off the winter cold. The first winter greens are ready to eat but, if you're lucky, there may still be some salad greens such as rocket and radicchio around. Apples and pears are still abundant and towards the end of the month the first satsumas, clementines and tangerines add a touch of brightness – and vitamin C – to the winter menu. If you eat meat, now is the best time for game. The pheasant season runs from October to February and you may come across wild rabbit at your organic butcher's. If not, try frequenting one of the growing numbers of farmers' markets to find these seasonal delights.

Focus: Poultry

Until the 1950s chicken and turkey were special treats. Today, they have become everyday fare. However, the price we've paid for our regular chicken and turkey dinners in terms of the

Organic poultry, like this turkey, move around freely and must have access to outside space.

birds' health and well-being, not to mention their taste, has been heavy.

Organic chicken and turkey may cost slightly more but the gains in taste and flavour more than repay the extra outlay – delicious, tasty white meat on the breast and full-flavoured, plump legs and wings. Above all, when you buy organic you can be sure that the birds have led longer, happier and more stress-free lives. Just choosing free-range is not always enough to ensure that this level of attention has been paid to the bird's welfare, diet and quality of life. Although, by law, free-range birds must have access to outside runs they can still, in some instances, be fed an unnatural diet and be reared in unnaturally large flocks of thousands.

By law, organically reared chickens and turkeys must have sufficient space to move around freely with access to outside space and fresh litter to scratch in. Contrast this with the conditions of intensively reared broilers, where often thousands of birds (up to 10,000 for turkeys and as many as 40,000 for chickens) are crammed into sheds or compounds with little or no natural daylight or room to move around. Newly hatched chicks in these intensive environments are put on top of a litter pile which is rarely, if ever, changed. They stand in their own mess and by the time they are taken to the slaughterhouse the litter has become a stinking heap and many birds will have developed ulcers on their feet from standing on it.

Organic poultry like Andrew Dennis's turkeys should be bred on traditional farms where they are able to roam in woodland or organic pasture land. Organically reared chickens and turkeys are also kept in smaller groups than conventionally bred poultry – ideally no more

Andrew Dennis offers some cooking tips along with his boxed turkeys at a local farmers' market.

than 500 broilers and layers and 250 turkeys per housing group and often far fewer. This allows them to develop a natural 'pecking order', which helps to allay the aggression and attacks that often occur between birds held in the crowded, stressed conditions of non-organic poultry sheds. Organic farmers are banned from beak clipping and other mutilations, which are often necessary to prevent intensively reared birds pecking each other. The use of antibiotics and other medicines is permitted only if strictly necessary, although young chicks can be given medicine to prevent a parasite infection called coccidiosis, which they're susceptible to.

Organic chickens and turkeys are fed on a nutritious, mainly organic, diet. Sadly, because there's a shortage of organic food at the moment, poultry can still be fed some non-organic food, but as more farms convert to organic production it is anticipated that the ratio will narrow. Even with this proviso, the diet organic poultry consume – consisting as it does of cereals, vegetable protein such as pulses, soya, vitamins and

minerals – contrasts favourably with that of non-organic poultry, which may well be fed on high-protein mixes that often contain growth-promoting drugs to achieve the biggest possible birds in the shortest possible time.

Organic birds are bred with their welfare in mind. They are reared more slowly, over a period of about 12 weeks as opposed to a typical six weeks or less for intensively reared birds. This gives them time to develop naturally and, because they have more space to roam, they develop healthy leg muscles. Most broilers are bred to have large breasts and get little exercise, and this leads to weaker leg muscles and painful problems for them, such as arthritis. The animals' welfare extends to the slaughterhouse, too, and organically reared birds are usually slaughtered on the farm premises. This avoids unnecessary and stressful transportation of the birds, and the more humane slaughter methods alleviate undue suffering. The sad end that most broiler birds meet consists of being shackled, upside down, on a moving slaughtering line.

Focus: Eggs

Many of us can barely remember the time when eggs came from farmyard hens fed on scraps from the table, and when poultry were allowed to scratch around and roam in traditional pastures. Eggs produced then, with their thick, hard shells, plump yolks, firm whites and exceptional flavour

There are battery, barn, free-range and organic eggs. All have differing standards of welfare, diet and quality of life for the hens laying them.

are a far cry from the mass-produced eggs of today, with their watery whites, over-yellow yolks and faint fishy tang.

The Soil Association's organic egg difference

Eggs and egg products carrying the Soil Association symbol (see p 100) must conform to the following key standards for poultry and they must:
• Have continuous and easy access to open-air runs during daylight, except in bad weather. Housing units must be moved to fresh pasture
• Have access to shelter and sufficient space in sheds to move around freely and be provided with litter to scratch in
• Be fed a diet consisting of a minimum of 80% organic food. The 20% of non-organic ingredients allowed must be guaranteed free of GMOs (see p 85)

It's anticipated that this will decrease in future as more organic feedstuff becomes available until 100% organic feed is given
• Have no more than 500 laying birds kept in any one shed, and often fewer
• Not be debeaked by an organic farmer
• Not use antibiotics routinely in feedstuff – it is prohibited, although antibiotics may be used to treat specific illnesses. During the time the bird is being treated the eggs cannot be sold as organic
• Not use artificial lighting to prolong days beyond 16 hours

All organic eggs are free-range, but a free-range label does not mean that the eggs are organic. Organic egg production aims to go back to more traditional production methods with concern for the egg-layers' welfare, and birds are allowed to range freely and are fed a primarily organic diet (with no colourings, designed to make the yolk a richer yellow, added). For taste and flavour there's nothing quite like a truly free-range, organic egg, but these are still not widely available. There is also still a great deal of controversy surrounding organic egg production as conventionally reared birds can be bought in at any time up until they are 18 weeks old and their eggs can be sold as organic provided they have undergone a 6-week conversion period.

There are several categories of eggs but, as with poultry, the image conjured up by the terms does not always match the reality. The majority of eggs sold in the UK are battery eggs. This means the hens are kept in large, airless, windowless sheds that contain tens of thousands of birds. Their unnatural conditions make them vulnerable to disease and they are routinely given antibiotics and other medications, as well as amino acids to enhance laying.

Although the term 'barn eggs' sounds cosy, barn hens are reared entirely indoors, too. Barns do have wooden perches and nesting boxes, and some have windows, but some are little more than glorified battery sheds and hens can still be desperately overcrowded with no room to move or fly.

In theory free-range eggs should come from hens that must have continuous access to the outside, at least via popholes. In practice, flock sizes can be so large that the more aggressive members of the flock dominate the popholes and bully the others, who remain inside. They may be

Check the standards

When buying eggs, be sure that they have been produced by birds that have led healthy lives. Do a bit of homework and seek out organic eggs, direct from the farm gate, an organic farm shop or from a small-scale producer. If buying them at the supermarket, make certain that they have been produced to the strictest standards of animal welfare. (If you have trouble finding organic eggs, the Soil Association (see address p 190) has lists of producers who sell direct. However, because demand outstrips supply they may not be able to meet the needs of all enquirers, but it's worth trying!)

little better off than battery or barn hens, and can in some instances be de-beaked, given routine antibiotics and fed diets that are far from natural.

Part of the problem is that shoppers are now used to buying cheap eggs, and organic ones are more costly to produce and thus more expensive on the shelf. We also want eggs all year round and organic egg supplies can vary, so there may be times during the year when eggs are less available and thus more expensive. Eating organic eggs, like so much other organic eating, means appreciating that there will be differences in availability, appearance and flavour and that demanding uniformity is unreasonable.

The box opposite is a guide to the Soil Association's prerequisites for organic egg production. However, not all organic eggs have been laid by birds that conform to these standards. Egg labels mean a variety of different things and, despite the cute pictures of farmyard hens on the box, what you see isn't always what you get.

FOR THE GROWER

Although the garden looks somewhat sad at this time of year, with the tattered remains of leaves barely hanging on to their stalks, there's lots to be getting on with. In areas of clay or heavy soil, now is the time to break up the soil by digging. This enables the frost and rain to penetrate, leaving you with fine, friable soil in the spring. Dig as much manure in as you can. You should also start your planting to ensure a good supply of vegetables in the year to come. Plant garlic, early peas, broad beans and new trees: fruit and nut trees and bushes.

Focus: Digging

Digging helps break up the soil, allowing oxygen in and water to drain away. It also enables you to introduce organic matter such as manure. November is the month to dig heavy, clay-based soils before the rain makes them too heavy to turn. Pick your day: the soil shouldn't be too dry or too wet, and as you dig pull up the roots of any perennial weeds. Throw the soil forwards from your spade or fork, leaving rough clods exposed to be broken down by the rain and frost. Weed seeds and pests are exposed, too, for birds to eat.

Chicory Castel Franco. Like your lettuces, covered in frames now, chicory can be forced in a heated greenhouse at this time of the year.

Sow early carrots now and protect them from the elements, if necessary, with cloches in their early stages. They are a real staple, and you'll nearly always find them alongside potatoes in your vegetable box deliveries (see p 68).

Garden jobs for November

- Sow early peas, broad beans, radish and carrots
- Cover lettuce, endive and parsley with frames
- Thin lettuce sown under cover last month
- Prune soft fruits if you haven't already done so
- Continue checking fruit trees, re-tie wall-trained fruit
- Sow green manures – grazing rye and field beans
- Remove perennial weeds by digging out roots
- Dig up rhubarb roots to force in your shed or greenhouse
- Start to force chicory
- Hang pieces of fat or fat balls on canes around fruit bushes – they attract insect-eating birds

Creamy turkey and bean casserole

This easy-to-cook casserole uses lovely seasonal vegetables like carrots and celery. It is an ideal way to use up leftover turkey from a turkey roast and it a real treat on a blustery autumn day. Serve with steamed organic rice or crusty organic bread to mop up the juices.

Preparation time: 10 minutes
Cooking time: 35 minutes
Serves: 4

1 tbsp organic olive oil
1 organic onion, chopped
6 smoked, streaky, organic bacon rashers
450 g cooked organic turkey, cut into
   large chunks
2 organic carrots, sliced
410 g can organic haricot beans
2 organic celery sticks, diced
150 ml organic white wine
250 ml organic chicken or turkey stock
1 organic egg yolk
150 ml carton organic single cream
1 tsp organic wholegrain mustard
2 tbsp chopped fresh organic parsley
Seasoning to taste

1. Heat the oil in a large pan and cook the onion and bacon for 3–4 minutes until softened, stirring often.
2. Stir in the turkey, carrots, beans, celery, wine and stock. Cover and cook over a medium heat for 20–25 minutes, stirring occasionally until the vegetables are tender.
3. Beat together in a bowl the egg yolk, cream, mustard and parsley, then stir into the casserole.
4. Heat gently without boiling for 1–2 minutes. Season to taste and serve with steamed rice or crusty bread.

december

Vinceremos, the organic wine specialists, is the brainchild of Jem Gardener and Jerry Lockspeiser. Always intrigued to know what leads people down particular career paths, I arranged to visit Jem to discover how he'd got into the organic wine business.

As the festive season was around the corner and plans for entertaining and catering had to be made, I decided to find out more about Vinceremos, who, among other things, supply the HDRA Organic Wine Club. The HDRA's Wine Club Midwinter Wines Case (advertised in their magazine *The Organic Way*) offers wines from France, Italy, Spain, Hungary and New Zealand and I decided to renew my acquaintance with Jem Gardener, the Director of Vinceremos in Leeds. We'd originally met when, in my capacity as Pat Archer, I'd opened an Organic Wine Festival at HDRA at Ryton.

The offices of Vinceremos Wines and Spirits Ltd (the mail order, trade wholesale and restaurant supply side of the business) and Bottle Green Ltd (linked with Vinceremos and selling to and supplying the larger retail outlets like the supermarkets) were, at the time of my visit, situated in the Bramley area of Leeds in a fine old three-storey listed building. It had originally been some kind of a mill, and also a cabinet- and coffin-makers' premises. Jem told me the businesses had sadly outgrown the splendid building and that they were on the move to gain extra space. Staff numbers have increased over the years from 5 to 20, with Bottle Green employing 14 and Vinceremos 6, so I could understand that things had become fairly cramped.

When I asked Jem how he'd got into the organic wine business he told me that the whole idea really began on a flight to Singapore. In the mid-1980s his friend Jerry Lockspeiser, who was then a youth worker (now his business partner in charge of Bottle Green), flew out to stay with his father, who was working in Singapore. Flying Aeroflot, he sampled Russian wine and vodka and, liking what he tasted, tried to buy it on his return to the UK. It was hard to come by and only available at one Russian shop in London, but he bought some and tried it out on his friends. They liked it and wanted to buy it, too, so he got hold of a few cases and began selling it as a hobby. The demand grew, and Jerry had the idea to set up a small business selling unusual drinks.

Jem was, at the time, working in a vegetarian restaurant but Jerry's 'Drinks with a Difference' idea appealed to him, so he let Jerry use a spare room at the restaurant as his first office. When the restaurant later closed, Jem went travelling for a time, but on his return he worked in an off-licence that specialized in quality beers, real ale and organic wine. He was particularly keen on the organic wines and recommended them to customers. Meanwhile, Jerry was still selling his 'Drinks with a Difference', and asked Jem if he'd be interested in joining him.

Farm shops, like the one at Pimhill, get their wines from suppliers such as Vinceremos, who import and distribute organic drinks.

Jem and Jerry decided to go into partnership, and the business became properly established in 1986. 'Drinks with a Difference' became a largely organic business. The stock of unusual wines from countries like Zimbabwe and Bulgaria sold well, but the organic ones did much better. Today, although the majority of the wines and other drinks they supply are organic, they do still sell unusual non-organic drinks if the demand is there. 'Moroccan wines sell quite well,' Jem informed me, and I noticed their catalogue carried an interesting (and reasonably priced) range from there.

Vinceremos supplies wines and beers nationally to restaurants, by mail order, through independent shops and of course via HDRA's Wine Club. They have a splendid catalogue, and the market is steadily growing. Jem is delighted with the growth in availability of organic produce, although he hopes the percentage of sales of organic wines and beer will soon begin to catch up with other organic products like dairy produce, meat, fruit and vegetables. Organic wine sales do lag behind. 'People don't seem to apply the same criteria when it comes to wine,' says Jem. In a recent survey of what organic food people are buying, beer came bottom of the list at 1%, with wine at 4%. 'Up to us to promote and distribute it better!' he says, but

Vinceremos is definitely doing its bit to promote organic wine. They are high-profile organic wine suppliers and there is only one other of any size in the country – many sadly went out of business as a result of the recession.

Safeway approached Vinceremos for supplies some years ago and it was this approach that was responsible for Jerry setting up the Bottle Green side of the business in the early 1990s. Bottle Green is an agency, brokering the wine and arranging to have it collected by customers. The agency now supplies organic wine to major supermarkets and some of the smaller ones, as well as off-licence chains throughout the country. Some of its aims are to be innovative and to promote newer and younger businesses.

Vinceremos imports the wines to a bonded warehouse and then sells it. Their warehouse in Burton-on-Trent (once an old railway building) is packed with stock awaiting distribution. Once, they did all their own deliveries, but increased demand has now made this impossible. Jem, although delighted with the growth in demand for organic produce, admits that he's some-times nostalgic for the somewhat rebel element of the earlier finge years. The name Vinceremos was chosen as a pun on the Spanish word *venceremos*, meaning 'we shall overcome', and well known to all involved in student politics in the seventies.

Although Jem goes abroad at least three times a year to visit wine producers and shows – where an organic presence is always newsworthy –

Some of the beers that are stocked at the Vinceremos bonded warehouse in Burton-on-Trent.

Organic wines are imported from all over the world and can be bought in many shops now or by mail order.

there was much more travel involved in the early days of the business, and a lot more tasting went on then, too. He is a wine merchant who stays loyal to his producers, although he is limited in where he can buy because all organic wine producers must be accredited (officially listed with a controlling body to prove their organic status). More producers are coming into the market, however, and Vinceremos add new wines to their stocks each year – about 50 new lines have been added in each of the past two years. Jem enjoys being an importer and distributor as he can have more control of his market, although, as he says, 'The disadvantage is that when a particular vintage runs out, customers have to wait till the following year.' With the soaring demand for organic wine, coupled with low yields in many regions of France during 1998, customers just have to be patient if stocks of certain vintages run out.

The organic wines advertised in the Vinceremos mail order catalogue have won many international awards, and have been much praised in the press for their high quality and, most importantly, their taste. To quote the catalogue: 'The image of organic wines as being weird, homemade or non-alcoholic has now been dispelled.' The wines have the characteristics and style of their own particular regions, and come from grapes grown without chemicals and pesticides. Organic wines are also low in sulphur dioxide which is a normal additive in wine-making (see p 185), and for customers prone to allergic reactions from wine, such as asthma or migraine, Vinceremos supplies information as to which wines are particularly low in sulphur dioxide. The catalogue also contains information about wines suitable for vegetarians and vegans, as wine is often clarified with 'fining' agents derived from animals (see p 185). The information is detailed and clear. Simple symbols are used, providing helpful advice on vintages, dryness and fullness ratings, alcoholic strength and which wines can be laid down. There is surely a wine there to suit every taste and occasion, with many at very competitive prices.

It seems that by far the biggest proportion of the wine they sell comes from France, with Italian wines taking second place. There are about 500 French organic wine suppliers, and that the number is growing at 5–10% per year. In Italy there are 200–300 organic wine producers, while in Spain the number has risen from only four a few years ago to around 14 or so today. For many years there was no organic Spanish Rioja available, but now there is a choice of about six or seven. Each country has its own certifying body, and in some cases there is more than one – 'France once had six, but is now standardizing,' Jem told me. England has one organic vineyard, Seddlescome in Sussex, producing vintages that Vinceremos can supply, and there's one Greek wine from Mantinia in the Peloponnese, as well as a good selection from New Zealand, Australia, USA, Hungary and Germany.

Jem very much likes some of the New Zealand Sauvignon, and he said he was also fond of Rhône Valley reds – in particular the award-winning Vacqueyras and some excellent Châteauneuf-du-Pape suitable for laying down. He said there was good Californian Zinfandel and Syrah, and that there are a number of very good red wines from the Tuscany region of Italy. Jem told me that there is a strong move nationally towards buying red wine. Organic red wine has always sold more than white, and they now sell approximately 60% red and 40% white.

The Vinceremos mail order list offers temptation to drinkers of every sort. In addition to the extensive wine list, fortified wines and port are available, as well as country wines from Broughton Pastures in Hertfordshire, which include blackcurrant, elderberry, elderflower, ginger and mead. Organic cider is available from Dunkerton's Cider Company in Herefordshire. There are organic fruit juices and cordials, and even olive oil and balsamic vinegar from Italy.

Wines with more traditional flavours are being produced with a variety of organic ingredients.

Jem said that the organic beer market has changed. The Caledonian Brewery, the last British brewery still using direct-fired open coppers, until recently produced Golden Promise and Golden Pale, but now only produces the former. Samuel Smith's brewery in Yorkshire produces a popular ale and has now introduced lager. Smaller UK breweries, too, are seeing a market for organic beer and those like Broughton Ales in the Scottish borders,

The supply of Dà Mhìle organic whisky, produced for the Millennium, sold out long before it had time to gather any dust in the Vinceremos warehouse!

who produce Organic Border Gold, St Peter's Brewery and Pitfield Brewery, along with the well-known names, like Sam Smith's, are all entering the market. As well as the British beers, there are also ones brewed in Germany and France. Spirits such as vodkas from Russia, Poland and Estonia and Cuban rum are part of the unusual Vinceremos stock, but as yet none of these are organic. However, organic gin and vodka made in Britain are now available. And in 1999 the world's first organic malt whisky was for sale. In the early 1990s a Welsh organic farmer called John Savage-Onstwedder decided to produce an organic malt whisky in time for the Millennium. He bought the organic ingredients and had the whisky distilled at Scotland's only family distillery, Springbank in Campbeltown. It was named 'Dà Mhìle', Gaelic for '2000', and 4000 bottles were prod-uced for worldwide sales. Despite its price tag of £60 per bottle, all Jem's supplies had sold out long before the whisky's release date in November 1999!

I asked Jem if, after a particularly stressful day, he wasn't unbearably tempted to tuck into some of the delicious sample wines scattered around the offices, but he said that although he does love wine he can resist it when he needs to. 'I found it much harder to resist the food when I was running the restaurant,' he said '… I don't think I ought to work with food again!' He very generously gave me a selection of wines to try, including a New Zealand Semillon–Chardonnay from Millton Vineyard, which was delicious, a splendid Italian Merlot and a bottle of Château la Garenne (a 1996 vintage Sauternes, which is France's top dessert wine).

I was very grateful to Jem for giving up his time to talk to me in the busy run-up to Christmas, especially as they were soon to move premises. Vinceremos is thriving, and Jem says that since the recession there are no really quiet times of year – they sell steadily all the time. He does admit that there is still plenty to do in order to increase organic wine's percentage share of the market. He joked: 'Maybe we should promote it by saying only organic wine doesn't give you a headache,' which may well be true when drunk in moderation. Aside from that enticing credential, the organic wine I've tasted has been delicious, so it can compete with non-organic wine for quality and flavour, too.

practical organics

Often one of the bleakest, coldest months of the year but, with Christmas on the horizon, it can also be one of the cheeriest. It's a time to take stock in the organic garden and for cooks to display their culinary skills.

What to try in
december

Vegetables
Broccoli *(i)*
Brussels sprouts
Cabbages
Celery
Chicory
Endive
Jerusalem artichokes
Leeks
New potatoes *(i)*
Marrows
Root veg: especially
  carrots, onions,
  parsnips, potatoes,
  sea kale beet, swede,
  turnips and winter
  radishes
Salsify

Fruit
Citrus fruit: (all *i*)
  especially oranges,
  clementines, and
  satsumas
Grapes *(i)*

FOR THE SHOPPER

Christmas dominates the month and brightens up the dull winter days by giving you the chance to feast on seasonal food. Order your organic turkey early to avoid disappointment and order a few other organic cuts, like beef, pork and ham, to supplement the table at Christmas, too. Seasonal vegetables include red cabbage (delicious with apple, and a change from Brussels sprouts with turkey), broccoli, leeks and Jerusalem artichokes (fantastic as soup or roasted with rosemary to serve with organic sausages). If entertaining, take advantage of organic convenience foods now available to make life easier.

Focus: Drinks
Wine

The demand for organic wines is soaring, and more and more vineyards are converting to organic production. Although organic wines often cost some 5–10% more than non-organic ones, increasingly people are choosing them for their better flavour and for the knowledge that they have been produced from grapes which have been grown for their character and quality, without the use of artificial fertilizers, pesticides and other chemicals.

The secret of a first-class wine begins with the grapes. Non-organic wines are produced from grapes that come from vines chosen for their high yields. The vines are intensively farmed with regular applications of chemicals to the grapes. In fact, staggeringly, although only a tenth of arable land in Europe is turned over to vineyards, they account for some three-quarters of all chemical pesticides and herbicides used. Not surprisingly non-organic wines contain pesticide and fungicide residues. According to the UK government's Pesticide Residue Working Party report in 1998, residues were found in 10 out of 72 samples (14%). Samples containing residues were from France, Germany and Italy and one of these, a fungicide (which is also found in pears) is thought to have an anti-androgenic effect – that is, it disrupts production of male sex hormones.

Organic grape growers, by contrast, choose vines on the basis that they have an affinity for the soil in which they are grown and a high natural resistance to disease and pests. They also use their waste products, such as grape skins, to make compost for use back in the vineyard, so completing nature's cycle.

Organic grapes are selected for their affinity for the soil and a high resistance to pests.

According to internationally acclaimed New Zealand organic wine-maker James Millton, of Millton Vineyard, 'The best quality grapes come from healthy plants which have harmony, balance and adequate natural water. The resulting fruit contains true ether (a compound in alcohol that makes it intoxicating) and is not interrupted with chemical sprays which can upset the yeasts and the resulting fermentation. The resulting wine is pure and clean and to achieve these ingredients it is obvious that the fruit should be grown organically.'

The other big difference between organic and non-organic wine lies in the production process, known as vinification. Organic wine contains much lower levels of the chemical sulphur dioxide, used in wine-making as a preservative to prevent over-oxidation of juice once the grapes are pressed. Sulphur dioxide is one of the chemicals thought to be involved in triggering a hangover. Many people report less severe hangovers when they drink organic wine, and this may possibly be because of the lower levels of sulphur dioxide. Sulphur dioxide has also been implicated in other conditions such as asthma, migraine, respiratory and skin disorders.

Non-organic grapes usually have cultured yeasts added to them during the wine-making process because their exposure to chemicals

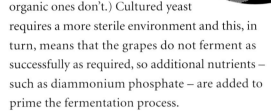

Said to produce a less severe hangover, organic wine often has a softer, fruitier flavour.

during growth reduces their levels of naturally occurring yeasts found on their grape skins. (Having said this, organic wines can have cultured yeasts added and some high-quality non-organic ones don't.) Cultured yeast requires a more sterile environment and this, in turn, means that the grapes do not ferment as successfully as required, so additional nutrients – such as diammonium phosphate – are added to prime the fermentation process.

Organic wine is allowed to contain some sulphur dioxide but levels are usually set at about a third of that allowed by the EU in non-organic wines. When less sulphur dioxide is used the juice oxidizes more, releasing more energy for yeasts to start fermenting. The resulting wines often have a softer, lighter, fruitier quality.

Sulphur dioxide also tends to lock up other chemicals, called phenols, in the wine giving it a bitter taste which then needs to be removed by 'fining' (or clarifying). Fining is needed in most wines to remove proteins, yeast residues, bits of grape skin and other particles that would contribute either to the instability of the wine or its lack of visual clarity. Fining uses agents that are often derived from animal products – egg white and gelatine (found especially in red wines), and isinglass (derived from fish bladders) and bentonite (especially in white wines). Most organic wines are fined, too, and, sadly for vegetarians, all the above agents are used from time to time.

TIP: WINES BY MAIL ORDER

Organic wines are available in off-licences, supermarkets and by mail order. Try Vinceremos or HDRA (see p 189) or The Organic Wine Co (tel: 01494 446557), Seddlescombe Vineyard (tel: 01580 830715) or Vintage Roots (tel: 0118 976 1999). Check catalogues for prices, varieties, availability and delivery, and keep a copy of your order!

Beer

Organic beers, lagers and ales are far less widely available than organic wines, although availability and variety are increasing. Most organic beers come from Germany and steadily more are coming from northern France. This is mainly because of a shortage of organically grown key ingredients – hops (most brewers buy them from New Zealand), barley and malt – and a reluctance on the part of British hop growers to go organic. At the time of writing there is only one commercial UK grower cultivating organic hops and a handful of British brewers (see pp 181–82).

As with wine, the superior quality of organic beer rests with its raw ingredients – the hops. Non-organic beers, lagers and ales are produced from hops that have been intensively farmed and exposed to high levels of chemicals. Organic hops, by comparison, are grown with a concern for the health of the hops and the environment.

Cider

Cider, once 'the wine of the west' has suffered from the intensive farming of the English apple orchards that has afflicted the fruit market generally. Organic cider is a real treat and very different from conventional blended ciders. Like grapes, the organic apples used for cider-making are chosen for their affinity for the soil they are grown in. There are an increasing number of fine-flavoured, individual organic ciders around now. Brands include: Herefordshire-based Dunkerton's (certified since 1988), whose range includes single variety ciders made from more unusual apples such as Breakwell's Seedling, Court Royal and Kingston Black. There's the Soil Association-award-winning H. Weston & Sons, also in Hereford, and Aspalls of Suffolk, one of the oldest organic producers in the UK.

Spirits

Organic spirits are still fairly hard to come by. Organic calvados (apple brandy), vodka and gin are available in some outlets. Currently there is just one organic whisky, Dà Mhìle (see p 182): it is made from 100% organic barley, using traditional floor malting. This involves laying the barley on a perforated floor to allow air to rise through it to enable it to germinate. It's a highly labour-intensive process but it produces a much finer-flavoured natural malt. The whisky is then aged in sea-aired sherry barrels before being filtered through a muslin cloth direct from cask to bottle. This preserves the natural fatty acids in the barley which are removed by usual filtration methods. The resulting whisky is cloudy if you add ice, but the flavour is more complex.

Non-alcoholic beverages

There are now lots of non-alcoholic organic drinks around including herbal teas, fruit juices, cordials and fizzy drinks. Keep an eye on the shelves as more are being introduced all the time. Because ingredients have not been exposed to high levels of pesticides and chemical residues, they are especially valuable for children.

You can get non-alcoholic organic drinks, too, such as fruit juices, colas and cordials.

FOR THE GROWER

It's often hard to get out in the garden now, but do finish preparing the ground for next year and tidy up generally.

Focus: Winter maintenance

To maintain an organic garden you need to be extra vigilant about basics like pest and disease control, and tasks like making compost and digging in manures. And, even in winter, you need to keep on top of the weeding!

Weed basics

The most essential factor in organic weed control is to start with 'clean' soil. You should dig it and remove as many weeds as you can. Some weeds, such as ground elder and bindweed, are especially persistent and you may have to make repeated assults on them to keep them under control. Burn perennial weeds like dandelion and ground ivy: if you put them on the compost heap, they'll take hold again.

Creeping roots from a neighbour's garden can be a real trial. To keep them at bay create a barrier. Dig the soil out just below the fence and nail a piece of board along it, then dig a trench, a metre deep, the length of the fence. Nail a strip

Check regularly on stored winter supplies.

of heavy polythene to the bottom of the board, with 15–20 cm overlapping the fence bottom and hanging down to the bottom of the trench. Backfill the trench carefully so the polythene stays vertical.

Inspecting the stores

Throughout the winter occasionally check any fruit or veg you have stored away. Remove any items that show signs of rot or disease. If they are left to fester, you may lose a lot more than just one apple, pear, potato or carrot.

Garden jobs for December

- Protect tender, soft growths from frosts
- Continue to blanch chicory and dandelions
- At end of month start to force rhubarb
- Prune fruit trees and continue to plant new trees, check ties, supports and stakes
- Keep greasebands sticky

- When the ground is not too hard, continue digging out perennial weeds and manuring
- Cover weed-free soil with a mulch
- Fill bean trenches with vegetable waste
- Check tools for repairs, clean and put away
- Order seeds for next year

By the light of the silvery moon

Biodynamic agriculture is a kind of 'superorganic' method of farming. Considered by many to be the cream of organic standards, it is used in over 30 countries throughout five continents and is particularly popular with organic wine makers. It avoids the use of chemicals and it sows and plants in harmony with the seasons and the universe. Developed by Austrian philosopher Rudolph Steiner, biodynamic farming works on the principle that animals, human beings, the earth and the universe are one united whole. According to this philosophy all sorts of natural forces, including the personality of the farmer or gardener and cosmic forces such as the cycles of the moon and the movement of stars, can affect the soil and the quality of crops. Biodynamic farmers use special biodynamic herbal remedies on their crops and soil to promote fertility and vitality, and they belong to the Biodynamic Agricultural Association. Their produce is marketed under the Demeter symbol (she was the Greek goddess of farming). James Millton, quoted in the Vinceremos catalogue, says, 'Biodynamics offers greater insights, helping us to know when it will be advantageous to take action with optimal effect… It makes us use our minds more – we learn to question why things are happening in the vineyard… We look to see what we can do to restore a balance by returning to the root cause of the problem.'

Plum syllabub trifle

This delicious trifle, which combines poached plums, almond biscuits and a syllabub topping, makes a fabulous alternative to Christmas pudding, or you could use it to end any special meal. You can make up to the end of step 1 the day before and then assemble the trifle before serving.

Preparation time: 25 minutes
Cooking time: 5–10 minutes
Serves: 8

100 g organic caster sugar
350 ml organic desert wine such as a Sauternes or Muscat, plus a little extra if needed
8 organic star anise
1 kg organic plums, halved, stoned and cut into wedges
55 g whole blanched organic almonds
200 g small macaroon biscuits
2 tbsp organic lemon juice
600 ml organic double cream

1. Put the sugar and wine in a heavy-based pan with the star anise and heat gently until the sugar dissolves. Add the plums, cover and simmer very gently for 5–10 minutes until the plums are just tender but retaining their shape. Remove from the heat and drain the plums, reserving the syrup and star anise. Leave to cool.
2. Lightly toast and roughly chop the almonds. Reserve 8 pieces of plum and all the star anise. Arrange the remaining plums in 8 individual glasses or a 2.5-litre glass serving dish. Scatter the biscuits and almonds over, then pour over 100 ml of the reserved syrup.
3. Make the remaining syrup up to 300 ml (by adding more wine) and stir in the lemon juice.
4. Whip the cream until just beginning to hold its shape, then gradually whisk in the syrup until the mixture forms soft peaks. Spoon the cream mixture over the biscuits and chill for 4 hours or overnight.
5. Arrange the reserved plums and star anise on the syllabub to serve.

USEFUL ADDRESSES

Book Contributors

Organic Farm Foods (Wales) Ltd
Llambed Industrial Estate
Tregaron Road
Lampeter
Ceredigion SA48 8LT
Wales
For information about whole-saling, retailing, importing and exporting fresh fruit and veg
tel: 01570 423099
fax: 01570 423280
enquiries@organicfarmfoods.co.uk
www.organicfarmfoods.co.uk

Rachel's Dairy Ltd
Unit 63 Glanyrafon
Aberystwyth
Ceredigion SY23 3JQ
Wales
For their newsletter or to arrange visits to the interpretive centre
tel: 01970 625805
fax: 01970 626591
enqs@rachelsdairy.co.uk
www.rachelsdairy.co.uk

Pimhill Farm
Harmer Hill
Shrewsbury
Shropshire SY4 3DY
For their regular newsletter or to arrange a walk of the farm trail
tel: 01939 290342 (office) or 01939 290075 (shop and café)
fax: 01939 291156
info@pimhillorganic.co.uk
shop@pimhillorganic.co.uk
www.pimhillorganic.co.uk

Henry Doubleday Research Association (HDRA)
Ryton Organic Gardens
Coventry CV8 3LG
To order the *HRDA Organic Gardening Catalogue*, their quarterly magazine *The Organic Way*, *HDRA News* or leaflets on composting, etc, or to become a member, get garden visiting times, book the restaurant or for

Heritage Seed Library or shop enquiries tel: 02476 303517
fax: 02476 639229
rog@hdra.org.uk
www.hdra.org.uk

Baby Organix
Knapp Mill
Christchurch
Dorset BH23 2LU
tel: 01202 479701
fax: 01202 479712
For comments, suggestions and any enquiries Freephone customer helpline tel: 0800 393511

Eastbrook Farms Organic Meat
Eastbrook Farm
Bishopstone
Swindon
Wiltshire SN6 8PW
For farm trail visits by arrangement and their regular newsletter, or orders tel: 01793 790460
helpline: 01793 790340
fax: 01793 791239
info@helenbrowningorganics.co.uk
www.helenbrowningorganics.co.uk

Duchy Home Farm
Head Office
The Duchy of Cornwall
10 Buckingham Gate
London SW1E 6LA

Hambleden Herbs and the Organic Herb Trading Co
Court Farm
Milverton
Somerset TA4 1NF
For orders by phone, or to order their mail order catalogue, arrange a farm trail visit or for general enquiries
tel: 01823 401104
fax: 01823 401001
info@organicherbtrading.com
www.info@organicherbtrading.com

The Village Bakery
Melmerby
Penrith
Cumbria CA10 1HE
For the shop, café and information about bread-making courses
tel: 01768 881515
fax: 01768 881848
admin@village-bakery.com
website: www.village-bakery.com

Whole Earth Foods and Green & Black's
2 Valentine Place
London SE1 8QH
For general information and enquiries tel: 020 7633 5900
fax: 020 7633 5901
www.wholeearthfoods.com

Woodlands Farm Organic Turkeys
Kirton House
Kirton
Near Boston
Lincolnshire PE20 1JD
For orders and enquiries
tel: 01205 722491
fax: 01205 722905

Vinceremos Wines and Spirits Ltd
19 New Street
Leeds LS18 4BH
For their mail order catalogue and general enquiries
tel: 0113 205 4545
fax; 0113 205 4546
info@vinceremos.co.uk
www.vinceremos.co.uk

Others

Biodynamic Agricultural Association
Painswick Inn Project
Gloucester Street
Stroud
Gloucestershire GL5 1QG
tel: 01453 759501

USEFUL ADDRESSES AND READING

Chase Organics Ltd
Riverdene Business Park
Molesey Road
Hersham
Surrey KT12 4RG
To order *The Organic Gardening Catalogue*
tel: 01932 253666
chaseorg@aol.com

Elm Farm Research Centre and the Organic Advisory Service
Hamstead Marshall
Near Newbury
Berkshire RG20 0HR
For research, advice and info packs for farmers and growers
tel: 01488 658298
fax: 01488 658503
elmfarm@efrc.com
www.efrc.com

Fairtrade Foundation
Suite 204
16 Baldwin Gardens
London EC1N 7RJ
tel: 020 7405 5942
mail@fairtrade.org.uk
www.fairtrade.org.uk

Irish Organic Farmers' and Growers' Association
Organic Farm Centre
Harbour Building
Kilbeggan
Co West Meath
Ireland
tel: 00 353 506 32563
fax: 00 353 506 32063

National Association of Farmers' Markets
South Vaults
Green Park Station
Bath BA1 1JB
tel: 01225 787914
www.farmersmarkets.org.uk

Organic Consultancy
A useful beginners' guide to organic food processing website for producers/manufacturers
www.organic-consultancy.com

Organic Farmers' and Growers' Ltd
50 High Street
Soham
Ely
Cambs CB7 5HF
tel: 01353 722398

Organic Food Federation
1 Mowles Manor
Manor Enterprise Centre
Etling
East Dereham
Norfolk NR20 3DY
tel: 01362 637314
fax: 01362 637980

Scottish Organic Producers' Association
Milton of Cambus
Doune
Perthshire FK16 6HG
Scotland
tel: 01786 841657

Soil Association Certification Ltd
Bristol House
40–56 Victoria Street
Bristol BS1 6BY
For advice and info, or to order their booklist or their *Where to Buy Organic Food* directory (with details of farm shops, box schemes and retailers, etc)
tel: 0117 929 0661
info@soilassociation.org
www.soilassociation.org

Terre de Semences
Ripple Farm
Crundale
Canterbury
Kent CT4 7EB
Call for details of their organic/biodynamic seed catalogue
tel: 01227 731815

United Kingdom Register of Organic Food Standards
Nobel House
17 Smith Square
London SW1P 3JR
tel: 0207 238 5605

Useful reading

Fork to Fork, Monty and Sarah Don, Conran Octopus, 1999

Gardening from Scratch 2, Gay Search with Helen Yemm and Jojo Norris, BBC Books, 1998

Geoff Hamilton's Paradise Garden Geoff Hamilton, BBC Books, 1997

How to avoid GM Food, Joanna Blythman, Fourth Estate, 1999

Organic Gardening, Geoff Hamilton, Dorling Kindersley, 1991

Organic Gardening, Pauline Pears and Sue Strickland, Mitchell Beazley/Royal Horticultural Society, 1999

Silent Spring, Rachel Carson, Penguin Books, 1963 rev. 1999

Small is Beautiful: a study of economics as if people mattered, E.F. Schumacher, Blond & Briggs, 1973 rev. 1993

The Food We Eat, Joanna Blythman, Penguin, 1998

The Living Soil, Lady Eve Balfour, Faber, 1943 (try your library)

The New Foods Guide, John Elkington and Julia Hailes, Victor Gollancz, 1999

The Organic Directory: your guide to buying natural foods, compiled by Clive Litchfield, Green Books Ltd/Soil Association, 2000

The Shopper's Guide to Organic Food, Lynda Brown, Fourth Estate, 1998

Whole Earth Cookbook, Hilary Meth, Vermilion, 1994

INDEX